THE
TOP 100
F1 DRIVERS
OF ALL TIME

TOP 100
F1 DRIVERS
OF ALL TIME

ALAN HENRY

ICON BOOKS

Published in the UK in 2008 by
Icon Books Ltd, The Old Dairy,
Brook Road, Thriplow,
Cambridge SG8 7RG
email: info@iconbooks.co.uk
www.iconbooks.co.uk

Sold in the UK, Europe, South Africa and Asia
by Faber & Faber Ltd, 3 Queen Square,
London WC1N 3AU or their agents

Distributed in the UK, Europe, South Africa and Asia
by TBS Ltd, TBS Distribution Centre, Colchester Road
Frating Green, Colchester CO7 7DW

This edition published in Australia in 2008
by Allen & Unwin Pty Ltd,
PO Box 8500, 83 Alexander Street,
Crows Nest, NSW 2065

Distributed in Canada by
Penguin Books Canada,
90 Eglinton Avenue East, Suite 700,
Toronto, Ontario M4P 2YE

ISBN: 978-1840468-94-6

Typeset and designed by Simmons Pugh

Printed and bound in the UK by Clays of Bungay

CONTENTS

INTRODUCTION

If you want a heated debate among motor racing enthusiasts, then just throw the name of the F1 driver you think is the best of all time into the conversation. That's surely guaranteed to turn a mild conversation into a blazing row. Michael Schumacher was the best! No way, it was Ayrton Senna! Haven't any of you guys heard of Gilles Villeneuve? So I suppose you were simply too young to have any memories of Jim Clark?

Even before I wrote the first words of the narrative, I was being warned by my journalistic colleagues that I was attempting the impossible. Correlating widely varied achievements across different eras would be unfeasible to the point where I would just be making a fool of myself. Well, yes and no. The qualities which made Bernd Rosemeyer such an inspirational sportsman in the halcyon days of Auto Union's ascendency are precisely the same as those which fire the emotions at the mention of Gilles Villeneuve's name. You may not be able to bottle star quality, but you can nicely factor it into a subjective assessment of any individual driver's record of achievement.

Let's just focus fleetingly on the top ten. I think I have offered adequate justification for the top four – Moss, Clark, Senna and Prost – in their profiles. With a combined total of 133 Grand Prix victories between them, they were obviously pretty good. Moss's versatility was astonishing, separated from the dynamic Clark by only a wafer-thin margin, but in the end it is Stirling who gets the nod – perhaps the nature of Jimmy's exclusive relationship with Lotus counts subconsciously against him. Whether in F1 or the supporting formulae, Moss drove a wider variety of different marques; but on the other hand, only Clark tried his hand at the Indy 500, winning America's most famous motor race in 1965. And Jackie Stewart came close to winning it in 1966.

Most recently, one must consider F1's latest man-of-the-moment, Lewis Hamilton. An outstanding talent with four wins to his credit in 2007, he's still a novice in statistical terms, so placing him 30th, just ahead of Nigel Mansell, ranks as a generous tribute to the most exciting new talent the sport has seen for years. If we return to revamp this volume in, say, three years or so, Hamilton should easily be able to make the top ten, even though it's not likely that the retired Mansell will be subjected to such a dramatic reassessment.

But before you start spitting tin tacks in outraged indignation at Michael Schumacher's 11th place ranking, just consider that the fact that you win should be matched in importance with how you win. I marked down Michael because of the contractual *droit de seigneur* which he imposed on his team-mates, even though it is clearly the way to win world championships. Anyway, I always had a soft spot for Mika Hakkinen, whom I still regard as an undervalued talent in the pantheon of world champions. If my bias shows in the final rankings, then so be it. No apologies coming there.

The issue of doing justice to team-mates is also a problem, apart from Senna and Prost in third and fourth places, of course. The late François Cevert, for example, is in 45th place and his old team-mate Jackie Stewart is eighth. In their last season together before Cevert was killed and Stewart retired, the Scot said his team-mate had the beating of him. Yet the record books remind us that Jackie won 27 Grands Prix and Cevert only one. So success certainly counts here, even though it is not the overwhelming factor.

Similarly, John Watson and Jody Scheckter may feel hard done-by in relation to their comparative placings with former team-mates Niki Lauda and Gilles Villeneuve respectively. But Niki and Gilles brought much more to the party than driving expertise, so there must be a 'premium benefit' for that achievement. In Lauda's case it would also be unfair if one failed to take account of the effects of his fiery Nürburgring accident in 1976, and his ensuing fight back from the edge of darkness to end up losing the championship to James Hunt by a single point.

There is, I suppose, an element of conventional thought when it comes to rating those two great contemporaries, Alberto Ascari and Juan-Manuel Fangio, but I grew up as a disciple of the late Denis Jenkinson, famed continental correspondent of *Motor Sport* magazine. He rated Ascari ahead by a whisker and I am happy to abide by his judgement.

I've included a smattering of great drivers from before the war, and some who never competed in the official world championship which was introduced in 1950. Ultimately, please remember, at the end of the day, that this book simply represents a personal opinion. Or at least, 100 of them.

Alan Henry
January 2008

THE TOP 100 F1 DRIVERS
OF ALL TIME

100. BRIAN REDMAN (Great Britain)

b. 9.3.1937, Burnley, Lancashire, England

12 Grands Prix. Career span: 1968 (Cooper); 1972 (McLaren); 1974 (Shadow).

Redman was one of the great sports car racers of all time. He was also an extremely versatile performer who was honest enough to confess that he wasn't really knocked out by the F1 business, and was happy to get back to sports cars after his dalliance with the Shadow squad in early 1974.

Brian's first F1 involvement came with the Cooper-BRM squad in 1968, when he suffered a badly broken arm after crashing in the Belgian GP, in the process of which his car vaulted the guard rail at the tricky Les Combes corner and crashed into a parked road car.

A brief sojourn in retirement in South Africa at the start of 1971 did not last long, and Brian was soon back on the international scene as a winning member of the Ferrari endurance racing team as Jacky Ickx's regular partner. A handful of F1 races with McLaren came his way in '72, but he withdrew from F1 through choice after a few drives for the Shadow squad, freely admitting that he preferred the less pressured environment of sports car racing.

99. JOCHEN MASS (Germany)

b. 30.9.1946, Munich

*105 Grands Prix, 1 win. Career span: 1973–74 (Surtees);
1974–77 (McLaren); 1978 (ATS); 1979–80 (Arrows); 1982
(RAM March).*

This amiable character was nicknamed 'Hermann the
German' by his McLaren team-mate James Hunt in the
mid-1970s, reflecting just what a good-natured relationship the two men enjoyed, although in truth it was
difficult for Mass to accept that Hunt was immediately
quicker than him when the Englishman arrived at
McLaren at the start of 1976.

Mass originally rose to racing prominence in touring
cars, most notably in the works Ford Capris which
contested the European Touring Car Championship in
the early 1970s, but he ultimately gained admission to
F1 on the strength of some competitive showings in F2
single-seaters. He made his GP debut for Surtees at
Silverstone in 1973, but switched to drive the Yardley
McLaren M23, vacated by the injured Mike Hailwood at
the end of the following season.

Paired at McLaren in 1975 with Emerson Fittipaldi,
Mass scored a half-points victory in that year's Spanish GP
at Barcelona's Montjuich Park circuit when the race was
stopped prematurely after Rolf Stommelen's Hill GH1
crashed heavily, killing four spectators.

Hunt's arrival at McLaren gradually forced Jochen
into more of a subordinate role within the McLaren
ranks. Eventually the whole situation rather seemed to get
on top of him, and he left the team at the end of the
'77 season. He switched to ATS the following year, but

suffered a disastrous season during which a testing accident at Silverstone left him with a broken leg, after which followed two seasons with Arrows and a final uncompetitive fling with the RAM March squad.

From then on, Mass enjoyed considerable success in Porsche sports cars, but he really deserved more from his time in F1.

98. STEFAN JOHANSSON (Sweden)

b. 8.9.1956, Vaxjo, Sweden

79 Grands Prix. Career span: 1979 (Shadow); 1983 (Spirit); 1984 (Tyrrell and Toleman); 1985–86 (Ferrari); 1987 (McLaren); 1988 (Ligier); 1989 (Onyx); 1991 (AGS).

This cheerful Swede certainly had all the right credentials when he finally graduated into F1 with the Spirit-Honda team in 1983. The winner of the 1979 British F3 championship, he was quick, brave and talented. He was also hugely unlucky, and despite spells with Ferrari and McLaren, never quite strung things together for long enough to claim that elusive F1 victory.

When Honda switched their engine supply contract to Williams in 1984, Stefan was reduced to accepting guest drives with Tyrrell and Toleman, finishing fourth at Monza in the latter machine while standing in for the suspended Ayrton Senna. He was lined up to lead the Toleman squad in 1985, but the team was unable to arrange a tyre contract. Another opportunity cropped up when Ferrari dispensed with René Arnoux's services after one race and offered Johansson the vacant seat.

Stefan ran competitively throughout 1985, and strong

second places in Canada and Detroit ensured that he was kept on the Maranello payroll in 1986. But that turned out to be a disappointing year and the Swede found himself replaced by Gerhard Berger in 1987, although a McLaren drive came up alongside Alain Prost in '87, albeit on the strict understanding that he was only keeping the seat warm in preparation for Ayrton Senna's arrival in 1988.

Stefan ran well in '87, but he was no longer in demand for a front-line F1 seat and his career gradually dwindled away on the world championship scene, although he would later revive it to good effect on the other side of the Atlantic.

97. PIERS COURAGE (Great Britain)

b. 27.5.1942, Colchester, England; d. 21.6.1970, Zandvoort, Holland

28 Grands Prix. Career span: 1967–68 (BRM); 1969 (Brabham); 1970 (de Tomaso).

Born into the famous brewing dynasty, Piers Courage was idolised by his friends in general and Frank Williams in particular, so it was one of the blackest days in the life of the British team owner when Piers crashed in flames and was killed in the 1970 Dutch GP at Zandvoort.

Was Courage good enough to be included in this list? His fans, of whom there are many, will say 'definitely'. Yet there was a time during his career when John Coombs, who briefly fielded an F2 McLaren for him in 1967, urged him to give up before he caused himself serious harm. Only a successful run in the '68 Tasman series, where he funded the cost of taking the McLaren to Australia and New Zealand out of his own resources, restored his professional credibility.

In 1968 Courage drove a works-supported BRM under the Parnell Racing banner, and also competed in an F2 Brabham fielded by Frank Williams. When Frank decided to make the big investment and move up into F1, Piers decided to go with him. Together they put on an impressive show, and the Williams team's dark blue Brabham BT26 duly carried Courage to strong second places in both the Monaco and US Grands Prix. Piers had entered the big time and proved that he'd got what it takes.

Buoyed up by these achievements, Frank Williams decided to expand his F1 operation for 1970, entering into a deal to use chassis supplied by the Italian De Tomaso company. It was beginning to show real promise in Piers' hands and was running mid-field at Zandvoort when he inexplicably flew off the road. The car erupted in flames and Piers never stood a chance.

96. TREVOR TAYLOR (Great Britain)

b. 26.12.1936, Rotherham, England

27 Grands Prix. Career span: 1961–63 (Lotus); 1964 (BRP).

Trevor Taylor made his name partnering Jimmy Clark at Lotus after Colin Chapman decided to get rid of Innes Ireland at the end of 1961. It was a thankless task for the pleasant Yorkshireman, who certainly proved very quick on occasion but who littered his CV with too many spectacular shunts for the team's comfort. In summary, second place to Graham Hill's BRM in the 1962 Dutch GP at Zandvoort represented the sum total of his F1 achievement.

Taylor had plenty of natural talent, but by the end of '63 seemed to have become a touch 'crash happy', and the notoriously unsentimental Chapman had no compunction about replacing him with Peter Arundell at the start of 1964. That left Taylor to join Ireland at BRP, but his best result was a sixth place at Watkins Glen in the US GP, and the team closed its doors at the end of the year. It marked the end of Taylor's career, save for his vain efforts to qualify the tatty Shannon-Climax for the 1966 British GP at Brands Hatch.

Trevor Taylor cut quite a dash in the F1 paddocks of the sixties with his bright yellow matching helmet and overalls. It is all too easy to forget that he was a talented performer who might have shone brightly in his own right, had he not been paired with a genius such as Clark.

95. EUGENIO CASTELLOTTI (Italy)

b. 10.10.1930, Milan; d. 14.3.1957, Modena, Italy

*14 Grands Prix. Career span: 1955 (Lancia and Ferrari);
1956–57 (Ferrari).*

This young Italian driver was fearsome, motivated, erratic and yet arrogant and arguably in over his head for much of his F1 career. That said, there was a sparkle to Castellotti's personality which made him attractive in the eyes of his many fans.

In 1951 he was an eager customer for a 2-litre Ferrari, which he drove without distinction on the Mille Miglia.

Cash was not a problem for him, or so it seemed; he came from a family of landed aristocrats. He was fiercely good looking, but, legend has it, vain to the point of wearing built-up heels in his shoes. In 1952 he ran second in the Mille Miglia before retiring and was offered a drive in the Lancia sports car team for the 1953 Carrera Panamericana, where he finished third behind Fangio and Taruffi. Finally, when the new Lancia D50 F1 car appeared in 1955 he was signed to drive as the third team member, alongside Ascari and Villoresi.

After Ascari was killed testing at Monza the week following the Monaco GP, Castellotti begged to be given a car for the Belgian GP so he could win 'for Ascari's memory'. Spa-Francorchamps was not really the ideal place for emotional gestures, but he hung on well in third place before his engine expired. When the Lancias were handed over to Ferrari in mid-1955, Castellotti went as part of the package, with the result that there were times at which it seemed as though the Commendatore had more drivers than he really needed.

In truth, the presence of Collins, Hawthorn and Musso on the team strength simply added to the pressure he was under, and in the 1956 Italian GP both he and Musso disgraced themselves in a blindly nationalistic battle which resulted in them both over-taxing their tyres and spinning off. By the start of 1957 it was Castellotti's personal life which was monopolising the tabloid headlines, due to his relationship with opera diva Delia Scala. While holidaying with her in Florence, he was summoned back to test the Ferrari 801 at Modena after Jean Behra set a new lap record in the Maserati 250F.

Clearly annoyed at having his holiday interrupted, Castellotti hastened back to Modena where, on the third lap of the test, he crashed into the small grandstand near the chicane at the end of the pit straight and was killed instantly.

94. JACQUES LAFFITE (France)

b. 21.11.1943, Paris

176 Grands Prix, 6 wins. Career span: 1974–75 (Williams); 1976–82 (Ligier); 1983–84 (Williams); 1985–86 (Ligier).

Laffite's irrepressible smile and infectious sense of humour helped brighten the F1 community for the decade during which he contested the world championship, but that apparent lightness of touch concealed an extremely professional racer who had great natural talent and came close to challenging for the world championship in 1981.

Jacques started his racing career as unpaid mechanic to his fellow French driver Jean-Pierre Jabouille and eventually scrimped and saved his way into the mid-1970s F3 community, winning the Monaco classic support race in 1973 and graduating into F1 with the Williams squad during the following year. Williams in those distant days was a precarious hand-to-mouth operation, but for rather more than a season Laffite struggled along with them, earning a crucial second place in the 1975 German GP which helped boost their cash-flow at a timely moment.

For the 1976 season Jacques was invited to join the new Ligier team, and he would stay there for several seasons, managing to score the marque's first win in Sweden during 1977. Two years later, Ligier swapped its Matra V12 engines for Cosworth V8s and Jacques harnessed the new ground-effect JS11 to superb effect, opening the year with wins in Argentina and Brazil and later adding the German race at Hockenheim to his personal tally.

In 1983 Laffite returned to Williams, by now a leading

team, where he would partner newly crowned world champion Keke Rosberg. In many ways for Jacques this was the happiest time of his F1 career, as he was a great Anglophile and he moved his family to the UK, renting the mansion at Stoke Poges which had once been owned by the Vanwall F1 chief Tony Vandervell.

Despite the fact that he was almost 40 years old at this stage in his career, Jacques produced some good drives for Williams in 1983, but the arrival of the Honda-engined FW09 the following year saw him drift away from a competitive pace and he was replaced by Nigel Mansell for 1985.

Laffite returned to Ligier, where the team was now equipped with Renault engines, and he produced some excellent performances in 1985 and the first part of '86. Unfortunately, a terrible accident at the start of the British GP at Brands Hatch saw him sustain two broken legs. Laffite made a full recovery, but his F1 racing days were now behind him.

93. STUART LEWIS-EVANS (Great Britain)

b. 20.4.1930, Luton; d. 25.10.1958, East Grinstead, West Sussex, England

14 Grands Prix. Career span: 1957 (Connaught and Vanwall); 1958 (Vanwall).

If one assessed Lewis-Evans on merit alone, rather than considering his modest record of hard results, he would certainly be placed much higher in these rankings, as, on his day, he could trade places with his more exalted Vanwall team-mates Stirling Moss and Peter Collins.

He was signed up in the role of third driver, cementing his position with a brilliant display of high-speed precision driving in the opening stages of the non-championship race at Reims, in the week following the French GP in 1957.

Lewis-Evans was a product of the cut-and-thrust world of 500cc F3 racing, and had risen to prominence through some drives in a Connaught and Ferrari sports cars. After graduating to the cockpit of a Vanwall, he rounded off the 1957 season with fifth place at Pescara and then second in the non-championship Moroccan GP.

Getting further into his stride in 1958, this small and rather frail-looking young man played a key role in Vanwall's onslaught on the constructors' world championship, finishing third at Spa and Oporto, and fourth at Silverstone. He displayed a high-speed touch and a great team spirit which was much appreciated by his more senior team-mates. Then disaster struck. Towards the end of the Moroccan GP – this time the final round of the championship – he crashed heavily when his Vanwall's transmission locked up and he sustained serious burns.

Stuart was flown back to the UK in Tony Vandervell's chartered Viscount airliner and was immediately admitted to the McIndoe burns unit at East Grinstead hospital, where he died six days later. The loss of this pleasantly unassuming driver hit Vandervell very hard indeed, and many people who knew the gruff industrialist believed he was never really the same man again after being touched by this tragedy.

92. WOLFGANG VON TRIPS (Germany)

b. 4.5.1928, Cologne, Germany; d. 20.9.1961, Monza

27 Grands Prix, 2 wins. Career span: 1957–61 (Ferrari).

Nicknamed 'Taffy' by Peter Collins and Mike Hawthorn in the mid-1950s, Wolfgang Graf Berghe von Trips was a dashing young German count, whose family lived in conditions of genteel if faded elegance on the family estates near Cologne, where he had been brought up.

This Robert Redford lookalike was offered his first F1 drive by Ferrari in what may have subsequently looked like a moment of weakness on the part of the Commendatore, as he crashed heavily on his debut outing in the 1956 Italian GP. It was only after the damaged Lancia-Ferrari was stripped down and checked over that it became clear that von Trips was blameless and his car had in fact suffered a steering arm failure like two of its sister cars in the same event.

Shrugging aside his reputation as a crasher, he won the 1961 Dutch and British GPs with a Ferrari 156, his car control and consistency in conditions of torrential rain at Aintree being simply remarkable, considering his unpredictable reputation. Poised to become Germany's first world champion driver years before Michael Schumacher was even born, he started from pole position for the Italian GP at Monza, but tragically tangled with Jim Clark's Lotus as the two cars braked for the Parabolica right-hander at the end of the second lap.

The Ferrari flipped up into the air, riding along the packed spectator fence, before slamming back onto the track. Von Trips and fourteen onlookers were left dead or dying.

91. RALF SCHUMACHER (Germany)

b. 30.6.75, Hurth-Hermuhleim, Germany

180 Grands Prix, 6 wins. Career span: 1997–98 (Jordan); 1999–2004 (Williams); 2005–07 (Toyota).

From his early days in karting Ralf Schumacher proved to be a talent, and that became obvious when he moved to cars, paving the way for a long and successful career in Formula 1.

His single-seater career showed all the signs of future stardom. He won the prestigious Macau Grand Prix Formula Three race in 1995, and then took the Formula Nippon title in Japan the following year.

He made his Formula 1 debut with Jordan in the 1997 Australian Grand Prix, which was also the first start for current team-mate Jarno Trulli. Incredibly, Ralf was on the podium in just his third Grand Prix when he finished third in Argentina, but that remained the best result of a tumultuous debut season.

A move to Williams in 1999 saw the start of what turned out to be a six-year stint with the team. In the first season with Supertec power, Ralf proved to be something of a revelation as a consistent points-gatherer, finishing in the top five no fewer than eleven times. The highlight was a second place at Monza.

In 2000, Williams began a new relationship with BMW. Ralf finished third in the new combo's first race in Australia, and went on to score two more podiums in the first season on his way to fourth in the championship. At the following year's San Marino GP, Ralf scored the first win for both himself and BMW Williams. After a difficult start to 2004, a heavy crash in the US GP side-lined him for much of the rest of the season. During his convalescence he was announced as a Toyota driver for 2005 and beyond.

He was passed fit to return to the last three races, making a point by qualifying and finishing second in Japan. He left the team at the end of 2004, having scored six wins and taken five pole positions. He had spent four of his six years as team-mate to Juan Pablo Montoya, and overall the pair proved to be very evenly matched.

Inevitably, it took Ralf some time to find his feet in his new environment at Panasonic Toyota Racing, and Trulli often got the better of him in qualifying. However, he impressed the team with his tenacity in races. He finished fifth on his second outing in Malaysia, and was fourth in Bahrain. Fortunately, another accident at Indianapolis, again a result of a tyre failure, was not as serious as the first. He bounced back to take his first Toyota podium with third place in Hungary.

At the last two races, Ralf found the revised TF105B more suited to his driving style. He took a superb pole position in Japan, and picked up another third place in the season finale in China. In total he finished in the points thirteen times in eighteen starts, and took an encouraging sixth place in the world championship.

The 2006 season proved to be less rewarding for Toyota, but Ralf scored an early third place after a superb drive in Australia. He finished in the points on six other occasions, including a fourth in France, to secure tenth place in the championship. He also qualified an excellent third in Japan.

90. ROY SALVADORI (Great Britain)

b. 12.5.1922, Dovercourt, Essex, England

47 Grands Prix. Career span: 1954–56 (Maserati); 1957–58 (Vanwall and Cooper); 1959 (Aston Martin); 1960–61 (Cooper) 1962 (Lola).

When I first joined *Motoring News* in the summer of 1970, the first character of note I was sent to interview was John Coombs, the Guildford-based Jaguar dealer who was one of the leading lights on the UK and European motor racing scene. During the course of our conversation, Coombs admitted to me that of all the drivers he'd watched who most deserved to win a world championship Grand Prix and hadn't actually managed to do so, Roy Salvadori came out at the top of the list.

From 1954 to '56 Roy handled a Maserati 250F owned by Sid Greene, taking a succession of good placings in predominantly non-championship events before being asked to drive for the works Cooper squad, and later the front-engined Aston Martin DBR4 which did not appear in the heat of the action until 1959. He later drove for the Yeoman Credit team, in whose Cooper he almost won the 1961 US Grand Prix. He was closing on Innes Ireland's victorious Lotus 21 in the closing stages when the Cooper's engine broke.

At the end of '62 Roy gave up F1, and he also abandoned sports car racing a couple of years later. A successful motor trader, he became heavily involved in the Cooper-Maserati F1 squad as team manager before retiring to Monaco in the late 1960s.

89. MIKE HAILWOOD (Great Britain)

b. 2.4.1940, Oxford; d. 23.3.1981, nr Tanworth-in-Arden, Warwickshire, England

*50 Grands Prix. Career span: 1963–65 (Parnell Lotus);
1971–73 (Surtees); 1974 (McLaren).*

Many students of motorcycle racing regard Stanley Michael Bailey Hailwood as the greatest rider of all time, but it was just a shame that his incredible genius did not quite enable him to make the transition to cars with the same level of success. Yet make no mistake about it, Mike the Bike proved himself to be a pretty handy single-seater driver, winning the prestigious European F2 championship in 1972 at the wheel of a Surtees and enjoying several highly impressive Grand Prix outings, including fourth and second respectively in the 1971 and '72 Italian events at Monza.

Mike first dabbled in F1 back in the early 1960s with the Parnell Racing team but then concentrated on bikes, his first love, for the rest of the decade. He later raced Surtees F5000 cars before making that F1 return, again driving for his fellow bike racer at the final Italian GP at Monza to be run without chicanes, at the end of 1971. The following year he was poised to make a bid for the lead of the South African GP at Kyalami when his rear suspension broke and he spun into retirement as a result.

Although Surtees and Hailwood had very differing temperaments, their background as motorcycle racers bonded them together in a workable alliance. Mike was genial, kind and totally devoid of any pretension, even though he came from a background of great wealth and privilege. Off duty and with a drink or two inside him, he could be quite a handful socially, but he was always highly professional about his driving. His bravery was beyond question, too, and he was awarded the George Medal for pulling Clay Regazzoni out of his blazing BRM at Kyalami, but the following year his F1 career finished for good when he suffered badly broken legs after crashing his McLaren in the German GP.

Mike retired from racing, but returned briefly on two wheels to win a sensational F1TT victory on the Isle of Man riding a 900cc Ducati, and followed that up by winning the Senior TT on a 500cc Suzuki. Then he stopped completely to concentrate on running his Birmingham-based motorcycle sales business with his old friend Rod Gould. And run it he did – it was like going into a Fiat dealership to find Michael Schumacher stepping forward to sell you a Punto.

After all this, in 1981 Hailwood was killed in a banal road accident, together with his daughter Michelle, when their Rover saloon collided with a truck on their way to collect a fish-and-chip supper near their home in Warwickshire. Few deaths have stunned the motor racing community more, nor left it reeling with such sincerely felt grief.

88. RAYMOND SOMMER (France)

b. 31.8.1906, Pont-à-Mousson; d. 10.9.1950, Cadours, France

3 Grands Prix. Career span: 1947–48 (Simca Gordini and Maserati); 1948–49 (Ferrari and Lago Talbot); 1950 (Ferrari, Lago Talbot, BRM and Cooper).

The son of a wealthy carpet-manufacturer from Pont-à-Mousson in the Ardennes, Sommer was three times French champion in the 1930s, sharing the winning Alfa Romeo at Le Mans in 1932 with Luigi Chinetti. Driving a works Maserati in 1947, he had a patchy season and spent some time away from the sport with illness, but he did drive the ill-fated CTA-Arsenal on its only appearance.

When Ferrari entered Grand Prix racing in 1948 Sommer was signed up as a works driver, being the first non-Italian to drive for Ferrari in a Grand Prix car of his own. That happened in the Italian Grand Prix at the Turin Parco Valentino in 1948. He remained with Ferrari for 1949, but half-way through the season he left to become a private entrant with a 4.5-litre Talbot Lago, finishing the year with a win at Montlhéry.

In the first season of the world championship, he came fourth in the Monaco GP in a Ferrari. He then decided it was better to run his own cars, and entered a Lago-Talbot in several Grands Prix, leading in Belgium before the car broke down.

At the Silverstone International Trophy meeting in August 1950 he drove the new BRM V16, but the car broke down at the start of his heat. Only a fortnight later, the man they nicknamed *Coeur de Lion* was killed when the steering failed on the Cooper he had borrowed from Harry Schell for the Haute Garonne GP at Cadours.

87. LUIGI MUSSO (Italy)

b. 29.7.1924, Rome; d. 7.7.1958, Reims, France

24 Grands Prix, 1 win. Career span: 1953–55 (Maserati); 1955–58 (Ferrari).

The death of this educated and cultured man as he battled to keep pace with his Ferrari team-mate, Mike Hawthorn, during the opening stages of the 1958 French Grand Prix, robbed Italy of its last front-line F1 driver of that decade. Born in Rome, Musso was the youngest of three sons of a diplomat who had served in China. 'Luigino' was not only a fine racing driver but also a capable horseman, fine shot and a fencer.

In the early 1950s his motorsport career progressed gradually as he climbed through sports car racing, first with a 750cc Stanguellini and latterly a 2-litre Maserati which benefited from a degree of works assistance. For the 1954 season he opted to move up to F1, purchasing a Maserati 250F in which he won the non-championship Pescara race, and he also finished second in the Spanish GP. After another promising year with the Maserati in 1955 he moved to Ferrari in '56, opening his association with the Prancing Horse by sharing the winning Lancia-Ferrari in the Argentine GP with home hero Fangio.

A crash in the Nürburgring 1,000-km sports car race saw him forced to sit out the balance of the season with a broken arm, but in 1957 he won the non-championship Marne GP at Reims. However, he increasingly found himself wilting under pressure generated by the rivalry with his two team-mates Hawthorn and Peter Collins as they went into 1958. The prize fund at Reims was reputed to be larger than at most races in Europe at the time, and there was speculation that he was banking on an infusion of cash to shore up a particularly speculative business enterprise. Perhaps he pushed too hard as a result.

86. JOHN WATSON (Great Britain)

b. 4.5.1946, Belfast

152 Grands Prix, 5 wins. Career span: 1973–74 (Brabham); 1975 (Surtees); 1976 (Penske); 1979–83 (McLaren).

All agree that this reserved and mild-mannered Ulsterman was a natural driver with great inborn skill, even though his perfectionist approach to the business of setting up an F1 chassis meant that he was often less than inspired if he failed to get the car working as well as he'd hoped. But when he hit the target, Watson could demonstrate world championship-winning potential, and indeed he was in with a chance of winning the '82 title crown, which eventually fell to Keke Rosberg in the final race of the season.

Watson was the son of a successful car dealer, and this funded his early racing career. Good performances in F2 racing and some useful sponsorship saw him enter F1, driving a Brabham in the 1973 British GP. The following year he drove for the Hexagon Brabham team and scored his first point at Monaco.

In 1975 he drove briefly for Surtees before signing up with the Penske team to replace Mark Donohue, who had been killed at the Austrian GP. The following year in Austria, Watson gave the team its first and only F1 victory. Penske quit F1 at the end of 1976 and Watson moved on to join Brabham, where he stayed for two seasons.

For 1979 he was recruited by McLaren after its intended signing Ronnie Peterson was killed at the end of the 1978 season. Initial hopes that he might have a chance of challenging for the 1979 championship collapsed when it quickly emerged that the new McLaren M28 was hopelessly uncompetitive and poorly engineered, a disappointment which unfairly kicked forward to have an adverse influence on Watson's reputation.

John's self-confidence was not exactly helped by his sparky relationship with team principal Teddy Mayer, and it was only when Ron Dennis and his technical director John Barnard intervened to calm the situation that the pleasant Ulsterman regained his equilibrium and started to deliver more representative performances.

By the start of 1982 he would find himself picking up the threads of his old Brabham driving partnership with Niki Lauda, a factor which perhaps slightly overshadowed his own efforts. Nevertheless, John drove outstandingly well to win the '82 Belgian and Detroit GPs. He then won again through the streets of Long Beach, but at the end of the year was dropped by McLaren.

After leaving F1, John drove sports cars for both Jaguar and Toyota as well as giving Eddie Jordan's first F1 car its preliminary shakedown at the start of 1991.

85. JARNO TRULLI (Italy)

b. 13.7.1974, Pescara, Italy

181 Grands Prix, 1 win. Career span: 1997 (Minardi and Prost); 1998–99 (Prost); 2000–01 (Jordan); 2002–04 (Renault); 2005–07 (Toyota).

Jarno first made his name as a world champion in karting, before finding success in German Formula 3 in 1996. Thanks to the patronage of Flavio Briatore, he made his Grand Prix debut for Minardi in Australia in 1997. He showed well in his early outings for the team before being invited to join Prost mid-season to stand in for the injured Olivier Panis. He finished fourth at the Nürburgring, and against the odds led in Austria in sensational style before retiring. Jarno had to stand down when Panis returned, but landed a full-time seat for the next two seasons alongside Olivier.

He struggled through some frustrating times with the French team, although on a day of high attrition he took second place in the wet 1999 European GP. He moved to Jordan for 2000, and immediately made an impression by qualifying on the front row at Monaco and Spa. In fact he started in the top ten on thirteen occasions, but had little luck in races and never bettered fourth place. If anything he was even more impressive in qualifying the following year, starting from the front four rows on fifteen occasions. Two fourth places proved to be his best results.

For 2002 there was a change of scenery as Jarno joined Renault. He outshone team-mate Jenson Button but was unable to add to his podium tally, with fourth place his best result. Things finally came together with a much more competitive package in 2003, when he also had a new team-mate in Fernando Alonso. Jarno scored his first podium in four years with a third place in Hockenheim, and twice started from the front row.

The 2004 season was a remarkable one for Jarno. He began it in fine style, regularly gathering points, and had the greatest day of his career when he won from pole at Monaco. Later he took another pole at Spa, but a series of frustrating races led to him leaving the Renault team after Monza.

Shortly afterwards his contract with Toyota was confirmed, and he was able to step into the car for the last two races of 2004. He gained valuable experience by finishing in Japan and Brazil, having started the former race from sixth place.

He began 2005 in great style with second places in Malaysia and Bahrain, and third in Spain. He also earned Toyota's first pole position at Indianapolis. In the second half of the season results proved harder to find. Nevertheless, in total Jarno finished in the points on nine occasions, and that ensured he earned seventh in the world championship, just two points behind team-mate

Ralf Schumacher. He shone in qualifying throughout the year, and on an average of grid positions he was ranked second, behind World Champion Alonso.

84. INNES IRELAND (Great Britain)

b. 12.6.1930, Kircudbright, Scotland; d. 23.10.1993, Reading, England

50 Grands Prix, 1 win. Career span: 1959–61 (Lotus); 1962–64 (UDT Laystall/British Racing Partnership); 1965 (Parnell Racing); 1966 (Bernard White Racing).

Had it not been for his well-defined sense of obligation, this extrovert and fun-loving Scot might well have enjoyed an F1 career punctuated by rather more wins than his sole success in the 1961 US GP at Watkins Glen.

After being fired in less-than-gracious circumstances by Lotus chief Colin Chapman, having scored the marque's maiden victory, he agreed on the spur of the moment to join the UDT Laystall team operated by Ken Gregory and Alfred Moss, father of Stirling, for the '62 season.

The following day he received an offer to join BRM alongside Graham Hill, which would have been preferable by far, although Innes was absolutely adamant that he should stick by his word and adhere to the original agreement.

Whether Ireland's rumbustious character would have sat comfortably with BRM boss Sir Alfred Owen, a strict Methodist, is another matter altogether. Certainly Innes liked a good time, but he was also a committed and very serious driver who hit the headlines in 1960 by twice beating Stirling Moss with the new Lotus 18 at Oulton Park and Silverstone. But Innes was always shrewd enough to appreciate just how good the new Lotus really was, and while he never seriously felt himself to be in Moss's class he was certainly audacious and frequently fearless.

Being dropped by Chapman in such an abrupt fashion left a lingering feeling of bitterness for much of Ireland's life, particularly as he mistakenly blamed his compatriot Jim Clark for having a hand in this dismissal. Sadly, the two men never made their peace before Clark's death in 1968. By then Innes had retired from racing, and in his new role as sports editor of *Autocar* magazine, he penned the most moving tribute to his fellow Scot.

Ireland subsequently severed all links with the sport and got involved in a couple of deep-sea fishing projects, neither of which yielded much in the way of commercial success. He later returned to journalism and enjoyed a spell as an immensely popular president of the British Racing Drivers' Club, before being felled by cancer in 1993.

83. TOM PRYCE (Great Britain)

b. 11.6.1949, Ruthin, Clwyd, Wales; d. 5.3.1977, Kyalami, South Africa

42 Grands Prix. Career span: 1974 (Token); 1974–77 (Shadow).

Tom was a contemporary of Brise, but if Tony was extrovertly confident, Pryce had a strain of Welsh reticence about him which made him appear shy at first glance, but which in fact concealed an impish, sharp sense of humour. This gentle son of a Welsh policeman won an FF1600 car in 1970 through a competition in the *Daily Express* newspaper.

He used his prize well and by 1973 was a leading contender on the British F3 scene, hoping to graduate to F1 the following year with the low-budget Token team, which eventually ran out of money just prior to the Monaco GP. Tom then back-tracked to take part in the Monaco F3 race which he won at a convincing canter. Within weeks he was recruited by the Shadow F1 team which was settling down into a steady tempo again after the tragic loss of their team driver Peter Revson, who had been killed testing prior to the South African GP at Kyalami earlier in the year.

Armed with the Shadow DN5 the following season, Pryce commandingly won the Race of Champions at Brands Hatch before qualifying on pole for the British GP at Silverstone, although he would slide off the track during the race. Pryce was another driver with intuitive talent; Shadow team manager Alan Rees reckoned he was a 'reflexes' driver like Ronnie Peterson, slightly inured to what was going on around him and unwilling to be involved in team politics. All agreed that Pryce had what it takes to make the big time, and he remained with Shadow to the abrupt end of his young life, despite efforts that Lotus made to engineer a swap deal with Ronnie Peterson in the spring of '75.

Pryce was killed when he hit a marshal crossing the track during the 1977 South African GP in what was one of the most bizarre accidents ever seen in the F1 business.

82. TONY BRISE (Great Britain)

b. 28.3.1952 Erith, Kent; d. 29.11.1975, nr Arkley, England

10 Grands Prix. Career span: 1975 (Williams and Hill).

In a sense you could say that we're getting into choppy water now, delving into the histories of those drivers who were little more than rising stars fresh out of the junior formulae, when events tragically called time on their careers. The perpetual dilemma is where to place them fairly within this complex overall picture without being accused of flattering unproven talent or, by implication, downplaying the status of more established drivers elsewhere in the list.

Yet Brise was unquestionably outstanding. The son of John Brise, a well known 500cc F3 competitor from the mid-1950s, Tony dominated the British F3 and Formula Atlantic championships before vaulting into F1 with the Williams team in the 1975 Spanish GP at Barcelona.

Brise then switched to Graham Hill's Embassy-backed team, and with the veteran double world champion formally announcing his retirement at the British GP, it seemed that the ideal set-up was being established, with Graham cast in the role of advisor and mentor to this bright-eyed young talent.

Yet the story was not to have a happy ending. On one foggy winter's night, Hill, Brise and four other team members were flying back to the UK after a test session at the Paul Ricard circuit near Bandol. Ignoring advice from the air traffic controllers that he should divert to Luton because of the poor weather rather than attempting to land at the much smaller airstrip at Elstree, Hill started to descend through the murk towards the fog-shrouded runway. But he was flying too low. His Piper Aztec brushed the top of some trees on the nearby Arkley golf course, then somersaulted to destruction in flames. All on board the plane died instantly.

Yet there was even worse to come. Hill's plane was

not properly insured, with the result that the bereaved families had to sue Graham's estate instead, a course of action which ended up leaving the Hill family virtually bankrupted.

81. RENÉ ARNOUX (France)

b. 4.7.1948, Grenoble, France

149 Grands Prix, 7 wins. Career span: 1978 (Martini and Surtees); 1970–82 (Renault); 1983–85 (Ferrari); 1986–88 (Ligier).

Arnoux started life as a garage mechanic at the French skiing resort where he was born, but his enthusiasm for cars and motorsport soon saw him secure a job with Conrero, the Milan-based Alfa Romeo tuning specialists. On the advice of Jean-Pierre Beltoise, who had just won the '72 Monaco GP, Rene's own motor racing career kicked off at the Winfield racing school at Magny-Cours, where he won the prestigious Volant Shell competition and moved into Formula Renault for 1973.

Tico Martini, for whom he drove in F2, then decided to build his own F1 car, but the resulting MK23 was a big disappointment because it did not feature the all-important ground-effect technology. The team failed to qualify in South Africa and Monaco but Arnoux made the field and finished ninth in Belgium. He raced on three other occasions, but lack of sponsorship caused the team to pull out of F1. At the end of the year he twice tried out the uncompetitive Surtees but failed to qualify on both occasions. He was, however, hired by Renault Sport for

1979 as partner to Jean-Pierre Jabouille, becoming a strong force, winning his first GPs in Brazil and South Africa and finishing sixth in the world championship.

The arrival in the Renault team in 1981 of Alain Prost changed things, and Arnoux won nothing that year. In 1982 he upset the team when he disobeyed orders and beat Prost at the French GP. It was clear he would leave the team in 1983, and the day before a deal with Ferrari was announced, Arnoux won again at the Italian GP.

In 1983 Arnoux was soon the leading Ferrari driver and that year won the Canadian, German and Dutch GPs to finish third in the world championship. In 1984, however, Michele Alboreto joined the Italian team and Arnoux was under pressure again. His performances became increasingly inconsistent and then, unexpectedly, he was ditched by the team just after the 1985 Brazilian GP. Arnoux sat out the rest of the year, getting his head back together again, and then returned to F1 with Ligier in 1986.

He was dropped by Ligier after 1988 and retired from the sport, and with Jean-Paul Driot established the DAMS (Driot Arnoux Motor Sport) Formula 3000 team. He has raced occasionally since his retirement, most recently in the GP Masters series.

80. THIERRY BOUTSEN (Belgium)

b. 13.7.1957, Brussels

163 Grands Prix, 3 wins. Career span: 1983–86 (Arrows); 1987–88 (Benetton); 1989–90 (Williams); 1991–92 (Ligier); 1993 (Jordan).

This cool and stylish Belgian driver admitted that he was inspired to a large extent by the example of his compatriot Jacky Ickx, and worked hard to develop a correspondingly smooth driving style as he learned the ropes on his climb through the ranks to F1. As soon as he was old enough to hold a driving licence, Thierry enrolled at a racing school, but his path to the sport's upper echelons was strewn with frustration and disappointment.

By 1980 he had successfully climbed through to F3 and taken over the works Martini drive vacated by the F1-bound Alain Prost the previous year. He finished second in the European F3 championship but then became somewhat bogged down in F2, first with a private March and then with the Spirit team.

Boutsen was understandably disappointed when he was passed over in favour of Stefan Johansson for the drive in the Spirit-Honda F1 challenger, but eventually he managed to get sufficient funds together to secure a seat in the Arrows squad. He drove for the Milton Keynes-based team for the next three-and-a-half seasons, developing a reputation as a precise, consistent and unflappable performer. That he was also extremely quick was not fully demonstrated until he moved to Benetton in 1987.

In 1988 he finished third six times in a season dominated by the McLaren-Honda turbos, and on the strength of this form was invited to succeed Nigel Mansell in the Williams squad, proving his quality and car control by winning the rain-soaked '89 Canadian and Australian GPs in fine style. In 1990 he added the Hungarian GP to that tally, driving just quickly enough to keep Ayrton Senna's McLaren bottled up in second place to the chequered flag. 'If you hadn't been a friend I would have had you off!' Senna told him on the podium, not altogether joking.

Williams were satisfied with Boutsen's pace, but by the middle of 1990 they were concerned that he really did not quite have the sharp edge of aggression which was necessary to carry the team to the next level. By then they were also in negotiation for Mansell to return to the team in 1991, for which a totally new FW14 design concept was being finalised in order to make a serious bid for their first world championship using Renault engines.

Thierry was extremely disappointed at this rejection and did a deal to drive for the Ligier squad for the next two years, first using a Lamborghini engine and latterly a Renault. But having parity of power units with Williams was only part of the story, and his F1 career effectively stalled in the slow lane at the start of 1993.

79. JOHNNY SERVOZ-GAVIN (France)

b. 18.1.1942, Grenoble, France; d. 29.5.2006, Grenoble

12 Grands Prix. Career span: 1967 (Matra); 1968 (Matra and Cooper); 1969 (Matra); 1970 (March).

The high spot of the motor racing career of Georges-Francis 'Johnny' Servoz-Gavin came in the 1968 Italian Grand Prix at Monza, where he was Jackie Stewart's team-mate in Ken Tyrrell's Matra International squad. After Stewart retired his Matra-Ford MS 10 with engine failure, Servoz-Gavin kept his sister car in the thick of battle to the chequered flag, and pipped the Ferrari of Jacky Ickx for second place behind Denny Hulme's McLaren.

Servoz-Gavin was one of France's most promising F1 drivers, but he competed in only twelve world championship GPs before retiring, after failing to qualify his Tyrrell team March 701 for the 1970 Monaco Grand Prix.

Born in Grenoble, Servoz-Gavin became known as 'Johnny' from his days as a teenage ski instructor on the slopes above his home town. With long blond hair and an easy manner, he developed a playboy image which he never shed.

Aged 21, Servoz-Gavin started competing in national rally events, but after attending the Magny-Cours circuit racing drivers' school he decided that he wanted to race single-seaters. He acquired a Brabham BT18 for the 1965 season, and his performances attracted the attention of Jean-Luc Lagardère, the Matra aerospace group's racing director.

Lagardère arranged a works F3 Matra drive in 1966 and Servoz-Gavin won the French championship. In 1967 he drove a Matra F2 car in the Monaco GP, but failed to finish, and the following year he returned to the streets of the principality, where he fumbled his biggest opportunity.

Jackie Stewart had been forced to miss the race with a damaged wrist. Team owner Tyrrell conferred with sponsor Elf, the French oil company, and Servoz-Gavin was made Stewart's stand-in. He qualified on the front row of the grid and burst into the lead. For three laps he dominated, then made a slip in the fast waterfront chicane and clipped a new guard rail with his left rear wheel. The previous year a similar mistake had killed Lorenzo Bandini, whose Ferrari flipped over and caught fire. Servoz-Gavin's only penalty was a broken driveshaft and retirement from the race.

In 1969 Servoz-Gavin won the European F2 championship for Matra and drove the experimental four-wheel-drive Matra MS84 in three Grands Prix. For 1970

Tyrrell selected him to drive alongside Stewart on a regular basis, but the team started the year with an uncompetitive March 701 chassis as Tyrrell wanted to keep using Ford engines: Matra would supply chassis only if Tyrrell switched to their V12.

Servoz-Gavin finished fifth in the Spanish Grand Prix but had been worrying about his vision after a tree branch struck his face while he was driving an off-road vehicle the previous winter. After again hitting Monaco's chicane and failing to qualify for the Grand Prix, he retired immediately, never to race again.

78. JEAN-PIERRE BELTOISE (France)

b. 26.4.1937, Paris

86 Grands Prix, 1 win. Career span: 1966–72 (Matra); 1972–74 (BRM).

This son of a Paris butcher won no fewer than eleven national titles in three years on motorcycles, before making his debut on four wheels with a 1.1-litre René Bonnet sports car in 1963. His career almost finished with a huge shunt in the Reims 12-hour race, from which he escaped with serious burns and a badly broken left arm, which would thereafter have only restricted movement.

However, Beltoise put his name in lights with a splendid victory in the 1965 F3 international at Reims at the wheel of a Matra, after which he moved into the international F2 arena with the famous French marque. He then won the F2 section of the 1966 German GP and rounded off his F3 career by winning all four races in the Argentine Temporada series the following year. By the end of 1967 Jean-Pierre had well established his credentials, and in 1968 he moved into F1 with the V12-engined car fielded under the Matra Sport banner, in parallel with Jackie Stewart at the wheel of the Matra International entry, which used a Cosworth Ford V8 engine.

The highlight of Beltoise's maiden F1 season was a splendid second place to Stewart in the rain-soaked Dutch GP at Zandvoort. Then in 1969 he was taken aboard the Tyrrell payroll as Stewart's team-mate, finishing second in the French GP at Clermont-Ferrand and then third in the Italian GP at Monza, where Stewart secured his first championship title with a split-second victory over Jochen Rindt's Lotus.

Matra missed the '69 season with their own V12 engine, preferring to sit out the year while they continued its development programme, but for 1970 and '71 they returned to the world championship fray. Beltoise drove with irrepressible gusto but never quite managed to nail a race win, even though he was regularly scoring points.

In 1972 the lure of team leadership attracted him to move to the once-proud BRM team, which was by now locked into a steady decline. Yet faced with monsoon conditions for the Monaco GP, Beltoise seized every opportunity and took every risk, thrusting his BRM P160 into an immediate lead at the first corner, and never looked back, delivering a bravura performance which left his competitors overwhelmed with admiration for the single-minded Frenchman's skill and tenacity.

Even Jacky Ickx, the acknowleged wet weather driver of his era, was almost half a minute behind with his Ferrari 312 by the time Beltoise took the chequered flag at the end of this remarkable wet weather masterclass.

Beltoise never won another Grand Prix and nor did BRM. The Frenchman used the ungainly P180 to win the end-of-season non-title race at Brands Hatch, and in 1974 bagged second place in the BRM P201 in the South African GP at Kyalami. Which was pretty much the end of the story.

Beltoise might not have been in the very front rank of F1 racing, but he was a dogged performer and worthwhile team player whose determination and versatility extended to some excellent performances in the Matra sports car team.

77. RICHIE GINTHER (USA)

b. 5.8.1930, Hollywood, California; d. 28.9.1989, on vacation in France

52 Grands Prix, 1 win. Career span: 1960–61 (Ferrari); 1962–64 (BRM); 1965–66 (Honda); 1967 (Eagle).

This small freckle-faced Californian grew up in the same bunch of aspiring racers as Phil Hill, who was a friend of Richie's elder brother. Richie's father worked for the Douglas aircraft company in nearby Long Beach and he briefly joined him in 1948 before making his racing debut in a Ford-engined MG TC hybrid that same year. However, on Ginther's 21st birthday all thoughts of a motor racing career had to be put on hold when he was drafted to Korea for two years' national service.

On his discharge from the forces, he partnered Phil Hill in the 1953 Carrera Panamericana before managing John von Neumann's Ferrari agency in California and then making his Le Mans debut in 1957 with a Ferrari 250TR. In 1960 he was invited to become one of the Ferrari factory's official test drivers, an opportunity he grasped with both hands. Following on from that, he made his F1 debut in a Dino 246 at Monaco in 1960 and that same year cemented his status within the Ferrari ranks by taking second to Phil Hill in the Italian GP at Monza, a race boycotted by the British teams in protest at the continued use of the bumpy banked circuit.

In 1961 Ginther was part of the 1.5-litre Dino 156 squad, personally putting in a tremendous performance to chase home Stirling Moss's winning Lotus 18, which was obviously a much more agile proposition through the streets of Monte Carlo. But at the end of the season he took the shrewd decision to sign for the BRM squad as Graham Hill's team-mate just at the moment that the British V8s were developing a properly competitive edge.

Reliable, consistent and a great team player, Ginther nevertheless lacked the hard edge of a ruthless winner and was replaced by rising star Jackie Stewart, who won the 1965 Italian GP just before Ginther, who signed for Honda, dominated the Mexican GP at Mexico City to win the final round of the 1.5-litre F1 regulations. He drove a couple of races for Cooper-Maserati in 1966 before the new 3-litre Honda V12 was ready, and was lucky to survive when the bulky Japanese machine spun out of control after suffering a rear tyre failure.

In 1967 Ginther signed to drive as the second man in the Gurney Eagle Weslake team, a deal which also involved a challenge at the Indy 500. He was waiting in the line-up ready to do his qualifying run at the Brickyard when he decided that he wanted to retire there and then, so he did just that without fanfare or fuss.

In 1989, now prematurely frail and unwell, Ginther was invited to the Donington collection, to become acquainted with one of his old 1.5-litre BRMs on the marque's 40th anniversary. He tried a few laps but it was all too much. A few days later, while on holiday in France, Richie succumbed to heart failure at the early age of 59.

76. EDDIE IRVINE (Great Britain)

b. 10.11.1965, Conlig, County Down, Northern Ireland

146 Grands Prix, 4 wins. Career span: 1993–95 (Jordan); 1996–99 (Ferrari); 2000–02 (Jaguar).

Eddie Irvine was not only a very respectable F1 driver, but he was also one of the shrewdest operators in the business, both on and off the track. A straight-talking wheeler-dealer who seemed to have a considerable amount of natural talent flowing from his fingertips, Irvine was clever enough to manoeuvre himself into the number two drive at Ferrari alongside Michael Schumacher. There he displayed just the right blend of deference and competitive spirit to ensure the relationship worked perfecly for both men.

After proving his talent in the cut-and-thrust of F3000, Irvine made his F1 debut for the Jordan team in the 1993 Japanese GP at Suzuka, where he infuriated eventual winner Ayrton Senna by repassing his winning McLaren after being lapped by the Brazilian's machine. After the race, a furious Senna stormed down to the Jordan garage and asked Irvine what the hell he thought he was doing. Irvine just shrugged, unimpressed and unbowed by the unwelcome attention he seemed to be getting from the sport's most impressive performer. Ayrton threw a half-hearted punch and Irvine half fell back over a table. The two men were pulled apart and that was an end to it.

In 1996 Irvine signed for Ferrari and immediately demonstrated a level of shrewd commitment and maturity, never failing to compliment Schumacher as consistently the quickest driver in the business and emphasising how much he could learn from him over the years ahead.

It was always tacitly agreed that Michael Schumacher should cement Ferrari's restoration as a front-running F1 force by becoming the team's first world champion since Jody Scheckter in 1979. That was the grand plan, at any rate, but on the opening lap of the '99 British GP at Silverstone, Michael slammed into the barriers at Stowe corner on the opening lap, breaking a leg in the process. Irvine finished the race second to David Coulthard's McLaren, and for the balance of the season the Irishman was locked in what amounted to an unintentional battle for the title crown, winning the Malaysian GP on Schumacher's return but then fading to third place in the final race at Suzuka where the drivers' title fell to McLaren's Mika Hakkinen.

Irvine won a total of four Grands Prix – all in 1999 – for Ferrari before accepting a multi-million-dollar invitation to sign for the newly branded Jaguar – formerly Stewart-Ford – squad in 2000, but despite some promising performances he was never quite able to help the team gel into a seriously and consistently competitive proposition.

At the end of the 2002 season, Irvine was negotiating for a return to the Jordan squad, but the deal never came together and Eddie gracefully quit the cockpit to concentrate on his worldwide real estate interests which, by all accounts, were as impressive as they were successful.

75. MICHELE ALBORETO (Italy)

b. 23.12.1956, Milan; d. 25.4.2001, Lausitzring, Germany

*194 Grands Prix, 5 wins. Career span: 1981–83 (Tyrrell);
1984–88 (Ferrari); 1989 (Tyrrell-Lola); 1990 (Arrows);
1991–92 (Footwork); 1993 (Lola-Ferrari); 1994 (Minardi).*

So tell me you've spotted the difference. Go on, don't be shy. That's it, we're getting stuck into the list of drivers I've ranked from 71 to 80 and you're finding that there's a common theme appearing: the further down the lists you go, the less successful a guy is – in ultimate terms, at least – then the nicer they become as individuals. OK, so I'll agree it's not a foolproof rule of thumb, but it's certainly worthwhile keeping in mind.

In a business which cruelly tends to erase memories of anything prior to last weekend's results, Alboreto cut a rather forlorn figure towards the end of the 1980s, almost as if he knew that his best days were behind him but he just couldn't give up hanging on to the reins of his involvement in F1, no matter how uncompetitive a car that might involve.

Watching this rather subdued fellow, his mop of curly black hair now flecked with grey, as he struggled with a succession of below-par machines, it was almost difficult to recall that this was the man who carried the 1985 world championship battle against Alain Prost through to September with a run of skilful performances at the wheel of a Ferrari.

When Enzo Ferrari originally announced his decision to sign up Michele for the '84 world championship season, he likened the young Milanese to Alberto Ascari and feted him in the role of the first Italian driver signed by the Prancing Horse in more than a decade. He would spend five seasons driving for the Scuderia, his silky smooth style yielding five wins before he fell foul of the team's legendary Machiavellian politics and was bundled out of the door at the end of 1988. He tried briefly to return to Tyrrell, but fell out with the team over clashing sponsorship deals, so then it was down the rankings via Larrousse and Footwork until he signed off after a year with Minardi.

Alboreto left F1 in 1994, aged 38, his fortunes having slumped after a twelve-year career . No longer wanted at the sport's highest level, but still passionate about racing, he switched to saloons and sports cars. It was while testing an Audi, in preparation for the 24-hour race at Le Mans, that he died, after his car somersaulted over a barrier on the high-speed oval section of the Lausitzring, a new circuit south of Berlin.

My colleague Richard Williams put it touchingly in the *Guardian*: 'Grand Prix racing is losing a sense of the value of its own history. But there are plenty of people who will continue to remember Michele Alboreto as one of the warmest men to drive the red cars ... as well as, on his day, one of the fastest.'

74. BRUCE MCLAREN (New Zealand)

b. 30.8.1937, Auckland, New Zealand; d. 2.6.1970, Goodwood, England

101 Grands Prix, 4 wins. Career span: 1957–65 (Cooper); 1966–70 (McLaren).

With a neat slice of historical symmetry, by taking second place in the 2007 Spanish GP, Lewis Hamilton succeeded team founder Bruce McLaren as the youngest championship points leader, being one month and two days younger than the New Zealander was when he won the 1960 Argentine Grand Prix at Buenos Aires at the wheel of a Cooper.

Thus in many ways, Bruce continues to bequeath the sport a remarkable legacy. Although only twelve years separated McLaren's arrival in Europe from his death in a testing accident at Goodwood, even now, some 38 years after his passing, his name remains a central element of the world championship business in one of the sport's most successful-ever racing teams.

Bruce would surely have delighted in the high levels of technical excellence and professionalism deployed by the current management, under the stewardship of Ron Dennis, although the current multi-million-dollar team headquarters near Woking, Surrey, is a far cry from the comfortable Auckland suburb of Remuera where Bruce grew up the son of a local garage-owner. In 1958 Bruce won the prestigious Driver to Europe award on the strength of some promising locally-run F2 Cooper races, and was taking the first steps on the road to fame and success. In 1958 he showed a lot of promise in F2 events in Europe, and he was promoted to the Cooper F1 factory team the following year, which saw him win the US GP at Sebring. This was followed in short order by the Argentine GP at Buenos Aires at the start of the following season.

For the 1963–64 Tasman series, McLaren set up his own team to run a pair of heavily modified Coopers and this effectively marked the start of the McLaren team proper, which duly made its debut in the 1966 Monaco GP.

By 1970 Bruce had established himself as a successful and prosperous businessman. There was talk of retirement from racing, a road car project was nearing completion, and the company was now a confident and viable business entity preparing to tackle the Indy 500. Bruce may not have been the fastest driver of his F1 era, but he was certainly one of the most consistent and dependable.

On 2 June all those plans were ripped apart with a terrifying finality. Testing at Goodwood with one of the latest McLaren M8D-Chevrolets, an insecurely fastened section of the car's rear bodywork flew backwards off the car at high speed. The car was pitched out of control, hit a disused marshals' post and Bruce was killed instantly.

73. PETER COLLINS (Great Britain)

b. 8.11.1931, Mustow Green, nr Kidderminster, England; d. 3.8.1958, Cologne, Germany

32 Grands Prix, 3 wins. Career span: 1952–53 (HWM); 1954 (Vanwall); 1955 (Maserati); 1956–58 (Ferrari).

The dashing Collins relinquished his chance of becoming Britain's first world champion in 1956, when he willingly handed over his Lancia-Ferrari to Juan-Manuel Fangio in the Italian GP at Monza. Having already won that year's French and Belgian GPs, the popular motor trader's son was now established as a world-class driver of formidable status. There was time enough to achieve his great ambition. Or so he thought.

Collins was not strictly obliged to make such a gesture, but the spontaneity with which he deferred to Fangio struck a chord among the appreciative Italian motor racing fans and also impressed Enzo Ferrari himself, not always a man to become overly sentimental about his drivers.

In 1957 Collins was joined at Ferrari by Mike Hawthorn and the two men quickly forged a close personal bond, getting involved in all manner of off-track pranks while obviously deriving huge pleasure from their motor racing. They nicknamed each other 'Mon Ami, Mate' after a character in a contemporary newspaper strip cartoon. Whether the pair of them actually concentrated sufficiently on the challenge of maximising their racing ability is another matter altogether, particularly when one considers the way in which they larked around while dicing for the lead of the '57 German GP at the Nürburgring, their antics surely allowing Fangio to catch their Ferraris at the wheel of his Maserati 250F.

Although Collins won non-championship races at Syracuse and Naples, there were no more GP victories coming his way in '57, but in 1958 his personal life perked up considerably as he married a popular American girl called Louise King. They made a golden couple, living an enviable lifestyle on a yacht based in Monaco harbour. Despite a shaky start to the season, Collins took the new Dino 246 to third place at Monaco and then built up the momentum of a world championship challenge with a decisive triumph in the British GP at Silverstone.

Two weeks later the Ferrari Dinos were really up against it, battling the smooth-handling Vanwalls over the bumps and undulations of the Nürburgring. Hanging on grimly to Tony Brooks's Vanwall, Peter pushed too hard at the climbing Pflanzgarten right-hander, spun off the road in a cloud of dust and bounced over the bank in full view of Hawthorn who was following close behind.

Hawthorn was worried sick but drove on like an automaton, anxious that his friend and team-mate had probably suffered serious harm in this awful incident. He was right; Collins had suffered serious head injuries, and despite being flown by helicopter to hospital in Cologne, he died shortly afterwards. It was left for Hawthorn to race sadly on and win the championship, becoming the first British title-holder and then retiring at the end of the season.

72. PATRICK DEPAILLER (France)

b. 9.8.1944, Clermont-Ferrand, France; d. 1.8.1980, Hockenheim

95 Grands Prix, 2 wins. Career span: 1972 (Tyrrell); 1974–78 (Tyrrell); 1979 (Ligier); 1980 (Alfa Romeo).

This little Frenchman grew up inspired by the example of his late compatriot Jean Behra and, like his hero, developed into a competitor who lived for the moment with the underlying belief that everything would work out alright in the end.

Yet this devil-may-care attitude thankfully did not work against his career prospects, although in truth it very well might have done. An example of this was seen by Ken Tyrrell in the autumn of 1973. Having been offered by Tyrrell the chance of racing a third car in the end-of-season North American races, Patrick broke his leg while messing about on a motorcycle. Thankfully that did not prevent Ken from inviting him into the team on a full-time basis in 1974, nominally replacing the late François Cevert, who had been killed practising for the '73 US GP at Watkins Glen, and who had been tipped to continue Jackie Stewart's winning tradition through 1974 and beyond.

For the next five seasons, Depailler repaid Ken's faith by developing into a loyal and audacious member of the Tyrrell squad, always giving his maximum and eventually being rewarded for his efforts with a fine victory in the 1978 Monaco GP. Then in 1979 he took the decision to accept an offer from the rival Ligier squad, winning the Spanish GP at Jarama before suffering serious leg injuries in a hang-gliding accident which sidelined him from the sport for the remainder of the season. This was a huge blow, as the latest Ligiers were clearly very competitive indeed, as his team-mate Jacques Laffite had so clearly demonstrated with convincing victories in both the Argentine and Brazilian GPs which had opened the season at Interlagos and Buenos Aires respectively.

Depailler struggled back to fitness for the start of the 1980 season when he joined Alfa Romeo, and had almost completely recovered from his injuries by the time he took part in a test session at Hockenheim in preparation for the German GP. A suspension breakage on the fastest part of the circuit caused him to crash fatally, robbing F1 of a driver who was totally committed to his profession through an abiding love of sporting values. To be honest, Depailler's crash indicated that there was still a scandalous lack of attention to circuit safety even more than a decade after Stewart's pioneering initiatives on this emotional issue. The catch fencing which could have saved Depailler – or at least minimised his dreadful injuries – lay neatly rolled up behind the trackside guard rails.

More than a decade later, his son Loic reached his 18th birthday. Asked by his mother what he would most like as a present, he replied that he would like a dinner party with all his father's former team-mates. It was an enormously popular and emotional reunion.

71. DICK SEAMAN (Great Britain)

b. 4.2.1913, London; d. 25.6.1939, Spa, Belgium

12 Grands Prix, 1 win. Career span: 1936–39 (Mercedes).

Assessing the status of Britain's most important pre-war Grand Prix driver with his later contemporaries is an obviously difficult task, made more complicated by the widely varying recollections of this wealthy Englishman, who died from burns sustained when his Mercedes hit a tree and exploded during the 1939 Belgian GP at Spa-Francorchamps.

Like Mike Hawthorn two decades later, Seaman was either lionised as a hero by his army of fans – or dismissed as a self-absorbed and boorish fop who was insufficiently consistent behind the wheel to be accorded star status. Yet the fact remains that Seaman was certainly the most accomplished British driver on the international scene in the 1930s, even if it was his wealthy parents' bank balance which ensured that he had the equipment necessary to catch the eye of the Mercedes team manager, Alfred Neubauer.

He was recruited for the 1937 season after winning four prestigious victories the previous year in his nine-year-old Grand Prix Delage, which had previously been driven by Earl Howe. Ironically, considering the impending hostilities with Germany, Seaman's parents had wanted him to pursue a diplomatic career, but even as he left Cambridge at the age of 21 in 1934, he was utterly and single-mindedly determined to become a racing driver.

On joining Mercedes his contract was personally rubber-stamped by Hitler, a measure of just how seriously the Nazi government took its investment in Grand Prix racing during the 1930s. Hitler had always been a fan of the British and would have had little in the way of reservations when it came to approving the deal. Unfortunately, little success came Seaman's way in 1937 and he had two quite serious accidents, one testing at Monza and another in the German GP. He was very disappointed not to achieve a good result in the first Donington GP, having been pushed off early in the race by an Auto Union.

Therafter he failed to win again until the 1938 German GP, a success which presented him with the embarrassment of having to give a tentative and half-hearted salute on the victory rostrum. Just over a year later came his fatal accident which was recalled after the war in painful detail by Hermann Lang, who emerged the winner of that tragic Belgian event.

'I will never forget the appalling sight as long as I live,' he wrote. 'The car had almost completely wrapped itself around a tree, the fuel tank had burst and Seaman was wedged in his seat like a stone statue, surrounded by a sea of flames.' Lang later added in tribute that he would always remember Seaman as 'kind hearted, cool and fair as a sportsman, just as I had always pictured Englishmen to be.'

70. DEREK WARWICK (Great Britain)

b. 27.8.1954, Alresford, Hampshire, England

147 Grands Prix. Career span: 1981–83 (Toleman); 1984–85 (Renault); 1986 (Renault); 1987–89 (Arrows); 1990 (Lotus).

A popular and gregarious Hampshire lad, by the early

1980s Warwick was regarded in some quarters as potentially even better than his contemporary Nigel Mansell, who would go on to win the world championship for Williams in 1992. Derek drove for the struggling Toleman-Hart squad from its F1 debut in 1981 through to 1983 and the experience was certainly character-building for all concerned, as the organisation – tiny even by the F1 standards of the time – performed miracles on their very limited resources.

Three years later, it was Warwick who succeeded the highly rated Alain Prost as Renault team leader and all the talk was about when Derek would win his first GP, or perhaps even challenge for the championship. At last he had the equipment beneath him which would enable him to run near the front of the field – or so it seemed at the time.

Derek looked as though he might win the season-opener in Brazil, only for his Renault to spin to a halt with front suspension failure after a brush with another car in the heat of battle. He also finished second in the Belgian and British GPs, but these were false dawns which offered a tantalising glimpse of what might have been rather than what was really to come.

In the end, events did not unfold as expected. The Renault RE40 was far from the competitive level he was expecting and the French car-maker's long-term commitment to the business of F1 racing with a works team seemed to be on the wane. Indeed, the team would be withdrawn from F1 at the end of the '85 championship assault and Warwick returned to F1 only mid-way through 1986 in tragic circumstances as successor to Elio de Angelis, after the Italian driver had been fatally injured in a testing crash with a Brabham-BMW at Paul Ricard.

Derek continued to drive with all the determination and confidence that had been his hallmark ever since the days of his single-seater apprenticeship in F3 a decade earlier, when he numbered the likes of future world champion Nelson Piquet as one of his regular competitors. After the F1 business abandoned him when he was dropped by Lotus at the end of 1990, Warwick moved into the sports car racing arena, first with Jaguar and then with Peugeot as the new decade got under way.

Family life and relationships were always of great importance to Derek, so when his younger brother Paul was killed in an F3000 crash at Oulton Park in 1991 it was a shattering blow to the tight-knit Warwick clan, particularly to the boys' father, Derry, who had supported them both with unconditional loyalty and commitment from the very start of their racing careers.

69. MARTIN BRUNDLE (Great Britain)

b. 1.6.1959, Kings Lynn, England

158 Grands Prix. Career span: 1984–86 (Tyrrell); 1987 (Zakspeed); 1988 (Williams); 1989–91 (Brabham); 1992 (Benetton); 1993 (Ligier); 1994 (McLaren); 1995 (Ligier); 1996 (Jordan).

Brundle was always a very tough competitor. Having cut his racing teeth battling wheel-to-wheel with Ayrton Senna through a nerve-wrackingly intense 1983 British F3 championship campaign, it was hardly going to be any other way. Truth be told, Martin was probably better than his CV indicates, for, apart from 1992 when he partnered Michael Schumacher at Benetton, he always had cars which were often not in the competitive front rank.

Moreover, Brundle was also pretty bold. Few drivers

have taken the audacious step to move away from F1 in a bid to enhance their reputation, but that's precisely what Martin did at the end of 1987. Frustrated with the lack of progress by the F1 Zakspeed team, he reasoned that a season of sports car racing in 1988 would do more for his reputation than bumbling around in tail-end hardware at the back of an F1 field. Twelve months later, he returned to the Brabham F1 team as reigning world sports car champion and in 1990 took another, similar sabbatical during which he won Le Mans, driving for Jaguar.

Brundle's best F1 season was undoubtedly 1992, when he occasionally managed to ruffle Michael Schumacher's feathers in equal cars, taking a terrific third place in the British GP at Silverstone. A succession of promising results led to a serious expression of interest in his services from Williams, but a prepared contract was somehow never signed and he drifted away to drive for Ligier in 1993.

Brundle's ultimate vindication came at Monaco, where he drove with great skill and concentration to keep Schumacher's winning Benetton running really hard in the closing stages. Martin was clearly hoping that the Benetton's Ford V8 might wilt, but it was very nearly the McLaren which failed to make it, the car's Peugeot engine blowing out much of its oil and water and only just about limping past the chequered flag.

After the race, Brundle and the Peugeot engineers were celebrating second place when along came Ron Dennis and sneered: 'Second is the first of the losers.' It was hardly what Martin wanted to hear after driving one of the very best races of his career.

After retiring from driving on a regular basis, Brundle forged an excellent career guiding the ITV coverage, first in collaboration with the legendary

Murray Walker, later with co-presenter James Allen. In that role Brundle has emerged as one of the sport's most measured and respected commentators, offering a balanced and straightforward account of events on the circuit which brilliantly connect with the casual TV viewer and much enhance the attraction of the UK coverage.

68. RUBENS BARRICHELLO (Brazil)

b. 23.5.1972, São Paolo, Brazil

249 Grands Prix, 9 wins. Career span: 1993–96 (Jordan); 1997–99 (Stewart); 2000–05 (Ferrari); 2006–07 (Honda).

On his day Barrichello could give Michael Schumacher a really good run for his money, but on the other hand there is a charmingly vulnerable side to this pleasant Brazilian, which seems to sap his motivation if things go badly wrong.

Barrichello won the 1991 British F3 championship ahead of David Coulthard and, despite a time-consuming detour into F3000 the following year, there were already expressions of interest in his services from F1 teams by the start of 1993.

Eddie Jordan duly signed up Barrichello at the end of the year, and very quickly he showed his class by running as high as third in the European GP at Donington Park, and then showing up his more experienced team-mates Ivan Capelli and Thierry Boutsen.

Barrichello scored his first world championship point at Suzuka, where he finished fifth, just ahead of his new team-mate Eddie Irvine.

The 1994 season proved to a nightmare for Barrichello. After two good results in Brazil and at the Pacific GP, he had a huge accident in practice for the San Marino GP at Imola. Two days later Ayrton Senna, his friend and mentor, was killed. It took Barrichello several months to overcome the effects, but at Spa he took pole position. A switch to Peugeot engines at the end of that year hardly helped the Jordan team and in 1995 results were hard to come by, although Rubens finished second in Canada. He stayed on at Jordan in 1996 but was only able to pick up a string of minor placings, although these took him to eighth in the drivers' world championship.

The relationship with Jordan ground to a halt and Barrichello headed for the new Stewart-Ford operation, for whom he took second place behind Michael Schumacher in the rain at Monaco in what was the team's fifth race. Rubens remained with Stewart for three years, taking pole position at the French GP in 1999 and scoring three podiums and a number of other placings to take seventh place in the drivers' title that year.

He then received the call to go to Ferrari as Michael Schumacher's team-mate. It was a tough job, but Barrichello was strong enough to cope and in July 2000 he took his first win in a German GP disrupted by a protester who wandered out on to the race track. He finished fourth in that year's title chase. In the years that have followed he has been a convincing number two at Ferrari, winning when Schumacher ran into trouble or when team orders allowed him to do so. This had increased his total of wins to nine by the end of 2004.

He left Ferrari at the end of a disappointing 2005 and signed to drive alongside Jenson Button in the Honda Racing F1 team. He stays with the team in 2008.

67. JENSON BUTTON (Great Britain)

b. 19.1.1980, Frome, Somerset, England

135 Grands Prix, 1 win. Career span: 2000 (Williams); 2001–02 (Renault); 2003–07 (BAR, later Honda).

When Jenson Button won the Hungarian Grand Prix in August 2006 it seemed as though he had finally made the long-awaited psychological breakthrough which would trigger a run of sustained success. For months afterwards he radiated the well-polished gloss of a winner as he sprinted to the end of the 2006 with a fifth, three fourths and finally a stupendous third place in Brazil after storming through from thirteenth place on the starting grid.

Yet Button's hopes that this momentum could be sustained into 2007 would be cruelly dashed. Honda continued to demonstrate a baffling inability to develop a competitive F1 car, and it was hard to see much in the way of bright spots on the horizon. Going into the British GP, while new boy Lewis Hamilton was aiming for a win, the 27-year-old from Frome said he would be satisfied if he grabbed a single point for eighth place.

Beyond question, Button is deeply frustrated about his plight, but knows full well that reversing an F1 team's fortunes is never the work of a moment. As the Honda management worked to recruit new staff – including ex-Ferrari star Ross Brawn and Williams chief aerodynamicist Loic Bigois – Button found himself trying to look past the problems in order to marshal his personal motivation.

Button is nothing if not scrupulously loyal to the Honda team, in public at least. He is not the sort of personality who generally allows his temper to spill over in public. When he wants to make a point to the Honda team principal Nick Fry and the engineers, he does so firmly and in measured tones behind closed doors.

Yet for the moment there is no alternative but to buckle down and make the Honda deal work, particularly as he reputedly paid in excess of $20 million to get out of a binding contract to drive for the Williams squad from the start of last year.

'Jenson really must get his act together this year, otherwise he's going to find the future very difficult, that's what it amounts to,' said Bernie Ecclestone, the Formula 1 commercial rights holder. 'But he really ought to stick with Honda to make it work, in my view. He needs to stick with Honda, get his head down and make it work. OK, so his current problems may not be his fault, and it's a shame they've happened, but he's just got to get things back on track.'

Nobody doubts Button's driving ability. 'If we at Honda can give him the car, which I ultimately believe we can, then there is no reason at all why Jenson should not be able to perform on the same level as Lewis Hamilton,' said Fry. 'He is a great team player and motivator.' Frank Williams added: 'I have always had a lot of admiration and respect for Jenson. He drove for us once and we wanted him to drive for us again. He is a fine competitor with a good racing brain.'

66. PATRICK TAMBAY (France)

b. 25.6.1949, Paris

114 Grands Prix, 2 wins. Career span: 1977 (Ensign);

Relaxing with a soothing cigarette, Bernd Rosemeyer looks unruffled and totally in command after winning the 1936 Italian Grand Prix at Monza at the wheel of an Auto Union. The superstar German driver, one of the most charismatic and popular personalities of his era, ranks seventh in this top 100 celebration.

Louis Chiron (left, 56th) and Achille Varzi (16th) celebrate together after sharing the winning Bugatti in the 1931 French GP at the Montlhéry circuit near Paris.

Hermann Lang rates 26th in this volume, largely on the strength of the talent which saw him win the 1939 European Championship for Mercedes. Had it not been for the war, he might well have been world championship material, but his best days were gone by the early 1950s.

Had he lived, Jean-Pierre Wimille (43rd) might well have beaten Giuseppe Farina to the first Alfa Romeo-led world championship in 1950, such was his pace in the legendary Tipo 158s in the immediate post-war years.

Rudolf Caracciola was one of the great pre-war Mercedes talents, arguably even greater than Lang, but post-war injury at Indianapolis in 1946 precluded him driving in F1 after the world championship was inaugurated four years later. He's rated 33rd.

Top slot in this informal and very personal assessment falls to the incomparable Stirling Moss … incomparable in the author's mind because of his matchless versatility and adaptability. He deserves star billing alone for still having his number readily available in the London telephone directory.

Tazio Nuvolari was another legendary name whose talent was definitely on the wane in the immediate post-war era. He ranks ninth in this assessment, mainly due to his Alfa victory in the 1935 German GP, which surely must rank as the outstanding jewel in his personal crown.

What else is there to say about the stupendous Jim Clark? Originally ranked fourth by the author, but promoted to second – only a whisker behind Moss – after a period of agonised and protracted reflection.

Jochen Mass's dazzling grin lit up the F1 pit lanes for much of the 1970s, but the affectionately nicknamed 'Hermann the German' never quite made the front line. Still, he scrambles in 99th in our ratings.

World champions both. Keke Rosberg (28th) shares a convivial drink with three-times title holder Niki Lauda, who earns 20th place in the listing between these covers.

Damon Hill gets comfortably into the top 100 in 39th place. Fans of the 1996 world champion may judge this too modest an assessment of Damon's talent – but he's five places ahead of his father Graham, who won the title crown in 1962 and '68.

René Arnoux's star shone brightly in the early 1980s and he looked like a potential world championship contender until dropped by Ferrari after only a single race of the '85 season. I rank him 81st, probably to the disappointment of his many fans.

*1978–79 (McLaren); 1991 (Theodore and Ligier); 1982–83
(Ferrari); 1984–85 (Renault); 1986 (Haas Lola).*

If there was any criticism to be levelled against this
charming and cosmopolitan gentleman, it would be that
he was probably too nice a guy to have the necessary hard
edge of ruthlessness to become a consistent winner. As a
result the debonair Tambay never quite reaped the hard
results his early promise seemed destined to deliver.

After serving a varied apprenticeship in the junior
formulae, his exploits earned him an F1 debut in the
1977 British GP at Silverstone, driving an Ensign entered
by wealthy Hong Kong enthusiast Teddy Yip. Scoring five
championship points in his first six Grands Prix secured
him an invitation to drive for the McLaren team as James
Hunt's team-mate, but by this stage the famous British
squad was running short of competitive momentum and
Patrick endured two lean seasons before being replaced
by Alain Prost at the start of 1980.

As something of a consolation he returned to his
earlier stamping ground in the USA, winning the Can-Am
sports car title in fine style. Although this was something
of a morale-boosting success, it was hardly the stuff of
which legends are made and, being just over 30, Tambay
felt there was still plenty of mileage left in him – but
closer to the world championship action.

Yet Tambay had not yet finished with F1. His route back
came via Yip's tiny Theodore team, after which he
switched to the Ligier squad following the mid-season
retirement of Jean-Pierre Jabouille, only to be dropped
again by the end of the season. Patrick's next F1 chance
came with Ferrari, filling the cockpit tragically left vacant
after Jacques Villeneuve's fatal accident at Zolder at the
start of '82. He drove beautifully to win the German GP at
Hockenheim on the day after Didier Pironi broke his

legs, then scored superbly the following year to win the San Marino GP after Riccardo Patrese threw his Brabham off the road in the closing stages.

For the 1984 season he was signed up to drive for Renault alongside Derek Warwick, a partnership which the French car-maker hoped would deliver some seriously worthwhile results. But like Warwick, he never quite made the magical breakthrough, although he very nearly won the '84 French GP at Dijon-Prenois after a wheel-to-wheel battle with Niki Lauda's McLaren-TAG which just exerted the upper hand in the closing stages of the race.

In 1986 he decided to gamble alongside Alan Jones to join the newly established Beatrice Lola team, which would be using a brand-new generation of Cosworth-Ford turbocharged engines, a deal put together by Indy team owner Carl Haas. It may have seemed like a good idea at the time but the whole programme ground to a halt at the end of the season, together with Tambay's F1 career.

65. RICCARDO PATRESE (Italy)

b. 17.4.1954, Padua

256 Grands Prix, 6 wins. Career span: 1977 (Shadow); 1978–81 (Arrows); 1982–83 (Brabham); 1984–85 (Alfa Romeo); 1986–87 (Brabham); 1988–92 (Williams); 1993 (Benetton).

The transformation of F1 racing's one-time *enfant terrible* into one of the most charming and gregarious personali-ties on the Grand Prix stage was a gradual process which took place over more than a decade. By the time he decided to retire after seventeen seasons in the cockpit, he had risen to the status of one of the most respected and highly regarded of competitors, gaining much of that esteem from his role as Nigel Mansell's highly competitive team-mate in the Williams-Renault squad in 1991 and '92.

After making his F1 debut for the Shadow team in 1977 he switched to the newly established Arrows squad for the following season, demonstrating a heady blend of brash aggression and considerable potential. His cocky manner put him at odds with many members of the F1 community and, in one of the sport's greatest injustices, he was wrongly labelled as responsible for the first-corner pile-up at the Italian GP which cost the life of Ronnie Peterson. He was later totally absolved of any responsibility, but not before the other drivers held what amounted to a 'kangaroo court' to ban Patrese from competing in the Italian GP as a punishment. All agreed that Riccardo was seriously wronged by this shameful episode.

Switching to the Bernie Ecclestone-owned Brabham squad for 1982, Patrese finally posted his first F1 victory at Monaco on the fifth anniversary of his debut in the sport's senior category. The following year he won in South Africa before spending a long time in the F1 wilderness, from which he was rescued with a switch to Williams in 1988. He stayed with the team through to the end of 1992, after which he switched to Benetton for a single season as Michael Schumacher's team-mate. During his years in the Williams enclave he was being measured against Mansell on a regular basis at a time when the Englishman was one of the fastest drivers in the world, and, in that respect, Riccardo was not found to be lacking. Only in really high-speed corners did

Mansell's sheer bravery yield dividends of fractions of a second.

Relaxed and self-assured, Patrese progressively developed into one of the most pleasant and even-tempered of individuals in the F1 pit lane. He also looks remarkably trim, and prides himself on still being able to fit into his original Shadow team overalls without any problem at all. Away from the circuits he lives a quiet family life with his wife Susy, his son and two daughters. More recently he took part in the short-lived Grand Prix Masters series, in which he proved that he had lost none of his professionalism and commitment behind the wheel.

64. LORENZO BANDINI (Italy)

b. 21.12.1936, Barce, Cyrenaica, North Africa; d. 10.5.1967, Monte Carlo

42 Grands Prix, 1 win. Career span: 1961 (Cooper-Maserati); 1962 (Ferrari); 1963 (BRM and Ferrari); 1964–67 (Ferrari).

He was undoubtedly the best Italian driver of his decade, although the even-tempered Bandini spent too much of his career in the shadow of his Ferrari team leader John Surtees. It was a role he fulfilled happily and apparently without any feelings of resentment, as he was, all attest, an easy-going guy with an uncomplicated disposition.

He married the daughter of a Milan garage-owner, and his father-in-law lent him a Lancia Appia Zagato in which to compete in the 1958 Mille Miglia. It was not his first event, as he had raced on occasion in 1957 in a borrowed Fiat 1100, but it was his chance to make an impression –

and a class victory on the Mille Miglia did exactly that.

He then bought a Volpini Formula Junior car, starting out on a path which eventually led to the chance to race an old Cooper-Maserati for Guglielmo Dei's Scuderia Centro Sud in the non-championship Pau Grand Prix in 1961, where he raised eyebrows after finishing third behind Jim Clark and Jo Bonnier.

He was recruited by Enzo Ferrari for 1962, although he did mainly sports car races. He competed in only three F1 world championship events, coming third in Monaco. He also won a non-championship F1 race at Enna in Sicily.

In 1963 Bandini was dropped from the Ferrari F1 team, but that spring he won the Le Mans 24 Hours, sharing victory with Ludovico Scarfiotti. He rejoined the reformed Scuderia Centro Sud and raced a works-loaned BRM that summer, qualifying on the front row in Germany, before being called back to Ferrari after Willy Mairesse was injured at the same event.

In 1964 he won the first Austrian Grand Prix to count for the world championship, held on the bumpy Zeltweg aerodrome circuit, after many of the other front runners succumbed with mechanical troubles, but for most of the time he was firmly number two to team leader John Surtees. His success in sports car races led to important wins on the Targa Florio in 1965 (with Nino Vaccarella) and in the Daytona 24 Hours in 1967 (with Chris Amon).

In the middle of 1966 Surtees walked out of Ferrari and Bandini found himself as the team's number one driver in Formula 1, supported by Mike Parkes and Scarfiotti. He led races but failed to win and by the middle of 1967 was under pressure, further exacerbated by the fact that rising star Chris Amon had been recruited as his new team-mate and he was now vulnerable from the New Zealander whom he both liked and admired.

At Monaco he was chasing race leader Denny Hulme when he crashed at the chicane and the Ferrari rolled and caught fire. Bandini was trapped in the car and suffered terrible burns, from which he died three days later. This was a gruesome and deeply unpleasant accident which was played out on televisions across the world, Bandini's only legacy to the sport being a heightened awareness of the need for much improved safety standards.

63. ELIO DE ANGELIS (Italy)

b. 26.3.1958, Rome; d. 15.5.1986, Marseilles

108 Grands Prix, 2 wins. Career span: 1979 (Shadow); 1980–85 (Lotus); 1986 (Brabham).

Civilised, cultured and impeccably mannered, Elio de Angelis drove racing cars with the same fluency and precision as he played classical music on the piano. He also seemed to have worked out how to stay just on the right side of that precarious divide separating consistently competitive performance from unnecessary risk.

With that in mind, Elio seemed the least likely of his contemporaries to risk death or injury at the wheel of an F1 car. Yet with all the poignant irony which runs like an undercurrent beneath the surface of this sport, when this Italian died in action it was due to a mechanical failure beyond his control.

De Angelis started karting when he was fourteen and quickly rose to international prominence. At the age of nineteen he jumped straight into Formula 3 and, at the wheel of a Chevron, won his third-ever car race at the

Mugello circuit near Florence. A fortnight later he finished second to Didier Pironi in the Monaco F3 Grand Prix, a startling performance. He later switched to a Ralt and added further wins that year at Monza and Misano. As a result he won the Italian F3 title at his first attempt. That year he also took part in a few Formula 2 races with Giancarlo Minardi's Scuderia Everest and led his first race at Misano Adriatico.

In 1978 he was offered the chance to race in F2 with a Ferrari-engined Scuderia Everest Chevron B42. Results were disappointing and de Angelis decided in mid-season to drop back to F3 and try to win Monaco again. He achieved this, and that led to a test for the Shadow F1 team in September that year.

Despite an offer from Tyrrell, in the end de Angelis ended up at Shadow with his father Giulio, a wealthy Roman building contractor, paying the bills. By the end of the season it was a different story, with Team Lotus keen to sign a deal with the twenty-year old. De Angelis walked out of his Shadow contract and joined Mario Andretti at Lotus. He was promptly sued by Shadow; but it was the right thing to do, and in his second race with Lotus he finished second in Brazil. He did not score again until the Austrian GP in the summer, but was then fourth at Monza and Watkins Glen.

He won his first race, a real nail-biter, at the Osterreichring in 1982, finishing just ahead of Keke Rosberg's Williams, and in 1985 picked up another victory after Alain Prost was disqualified at Imola. By now, however, Ayrton Senna had joined Lotus and it was clear that if de Angelis wanted to stay, he would have to do so as the number two.

In 1986 he moved to Brabham, where he was joined by his compatriot Riccardo Patrese. The team ran the ultra-lowline BMW-engined BT55, the final Brabham design concept to be pioneered by Gordon Murray, and it was while testing this in May at Paul Ricard that he received fatal injuries when a rear wing failed.

62. STEFAN BELLOF (Germany)

b. 20.11.1957, Giessen, Germany; d. 1.9.1985, Spa-Francorchamps

20 Grands Prix. Career span: 1984–85 (Tyrrell).

The original intention of this book was to write a succession of 500-word cameos on the 100 drivers concerned, but how do you string the story out long enough to do justice to Stefan Bellof? The young German's name is largely forgotten since he briefly flashed across the F1 horizon some 23 years ago, but for those who attended the 1984 Monaco GP here was a talent right up there with Ayrton Senna, who up to that point had been regarded as the sport's most exciting new talent.

In summary, Bellof was a spectacular, Rindt-like talent who exploded into prominence when he scored a brace of F2 victories early in 1983 at the wheel of a Maurer-BMW. He joined Tyrrell the following year and, at the height of that season's Monaco GP monsoon, was running in a strong third place, closing in on Prost's leading McLaren and Senna's second-place Toleman when the race was flagged to a premature halt as the conditions became impossible. Unfortunately, both he and his team-mate Martin Brundle were forced to sit out the second half of the '84 season after Tyrrell were suspended from the championship following the Englishman's exclusion from second place in the Detroit GP after it was – incorrectly – judged that his fuel was using illegal additives.

Of course, as far as Bellof was concerned, just where his career path might have led him had he won the most famous race on the F1 calendar at his first attempt is anybody's guess. Tragically, he was killed at Spa when he tried to force his Porsche 962 into the lead of the 1,000-km sports car race ahead of Jacky Ickx's sister car and slammed head-on into a trackside barrier at 150mph.

61. FROILAN GONZALEZ (Argentina)

b. 5.10.1922, Arrecifes, Argentina

26 Grands Prix, 2 wins. Career span: 1950 (Maserati); 1951 (Talbot and Ferrari); 1952–53 (Maserati); 1954–55 (Ferrari); 1956 (Maserati and Vanwall); 1957 (Ferrari); 1960 (Ferrari).

At the time of writing (December 2007) José Froilan Gonzalez is the sport's oldest surviving world championship Grand Prix winner, having scored Ferrari's first such success with victory in the 1951 British GP at Silverstone. Enzo Ferrari reportedly once expressed a degree of amazement over how the chubby Gonzalez – a close friend and contemporary of the legendary Juan-Manuel Fangio – drove racing cars so effectively, such was the lather he seemed to work himself into.

Gonzalez was nicknamed 'The Pampas Bull' by members of the British motor racing community, the same souls who inexplicably called Wolfgang von Trips 'Taffy' when he drove for Ferrari later in the championship's opening decade. His compatriots affectionately called him 'El Cabezon' (Fat Head), but he was far from unfit by any objective standards.

The son of a Chevrolet dealer from provincial Argentina, Gonzalez was a chubby baby who grew into a chubby man. Yet he was also a keen all-round sportsman: a first-rate swimmer, a crack shot, a cyclist and a production car road racer just like Fangio had been. His father set him up in the trucking business and by 1949 he was ready to join Fangio on the European tour.

During his first couple of seasons, results were rather hard to come by, but when Mercedes took a trio of their outdated pre-war W163s to race in Argentina, Gonzalez hit the headlines by beating them on the Costanera circuit in a supercharged 2-litre Ferrari 166, setting himself up for the works Ferrari drive which would put his name up in lights at Silverstone a few months later. He drove for Maserati in 1953, then went back to Ferrari in '54, when he again won the British GP at Silverstone for the Prancing Horse.

Later that season Gonzalez crashed a Ferrari sports car in practice for the Tourist Trophy and only once again drove an F1 car in the UK, a Vanwall in the '56 British GP at Silverstone which broke a driveshaft joint on the startline.

Gonzalez's final F1 outing came at the wheel of a Ferrari Dino 246 in the 1960 Argentine GP at Buenos Aires, where he finished tenth in a race which saw his team-mate Cliff Allison post a splendid second place behind Bruce McLaren's winning Cooper-Climax.

60. FELIPE MASSA (Brazil)

b. 25.4.1981, São Paolo, Brazil

87 Grands Prix, 5 wins. Career span: 2002, 2004–05 (Sauber); 2006–07 (Ferrari).

There is an uncomplicated, twinkling charm about Felipe Massa which somehow tempts you to look past his obvious role as a world championship contender. The relaxed Brazilian's easy demeanour makes him look like a bloke who likes driving racing cars and somehow could not quite believe that he'd landed a Ferrari drive in 2006 as one of the key claimants to the legendary Michael Schumacher's crown.

Yet his hard on-track achievements have served to contradict this slightly soft, rather tactile image. Massa is maturing into a tough customer, as Fernando Alonso found out to his cost when he tried sitting it out, wheel-to-wheel, with the Ferrari driver going into the first corner in the 2007 Spanish Grand Prix.

Massa's emergence as a title contender in 2007 left the paddock divided. There are those who believed that he would immediately be overshadowed by the prodigiously talented Kimi Raikkonen, the super-fast Finn who moved from McLaren to succeed Schumacher at the end of the '05 season. Yet although Raikkonen won the opening race of the season in Melbourne, he took time to gain the upper hand over Massa, something many thought would be little more than a formality.

Others believe that Felipe has retrospectively validated his 2006 performances as Schumacher's running mate and that the pace he demonstrated alongside the seven-times world champion now looks like a genuine reflection of his speed and ability.

Ironically, it was Massa's lowest moment of the 2007 season that seems to have been the making of him. In Malaysia he qualified his Ferrari superbly on pole position, but lost out to eventual winner Fernando Alonso's McLaren on the sprint down to the first corner before making a series of mistakes battling with Lewis Hamilton and eventually trailing home a crestfallen fifth.

There was only a week's break between Malaysia and the third round in Bahrain, seven days for Massa to wait before gaining the opportunity to atone, seven days during which he bore the brunt of media criticism calling into question his suitability for the exacting role of a Ferrari driver. He answered his critics by winning first in Bahrain, then again in Spain, the next race on the calendar.

'I learned a lot from Michael from the moment I became test driver with Ferrari,' he said. 'Then in the second half of last year I found that I was able to stay close to his pace as he was battling for the world championship. What he taught me was not so much about driving technique or lapping quickly, but more about the importance of being totally focused, fit and single-minded as you need to be if you are going to have a chance of winning the world championship.'

So how does Massa feel about the prospect of joining Emerson Fittipaldi, Nelson Piquet and Ayrton Senna in the pantheon of Brazilian greats as only his country's fourth-ever world champion?

He responded with another flash of that impish grin. 'Well, when I won at Interlagos [in '06] for Ferrari at the end of last year I experienced the joy of the Brazilian public,' he said. 'I certainly know what they are expecting of me, but I don't feel that desire in terms of hard pressure.'

ALAN HENRY

59. DAVID COULTHARD (Great Britain)

b. 27.3.1971, Twynholm, Scotland

228 Grands Prix, 13 wins. Career span: 1994–95 (Williams); 1996–2004 (McLaren); 2005–07 (Red Bull).

Probably best not to remind David Coulthard that if he'd stayed with Williams in 1996 rather than moving to McLaren, he might well have won the world championship which eventually fell to his former team-mate Damon Hill. As it was, the popular and personable Scot had to settle for a career-best second place in the 2001 title chase behind Ferrari ace Michael Schumacher.

Nominated as the official Williams test driver in 1994, Coulthard stepped into the limelight after Ayrton Senna was killed in that year's San Marino GP. Only an ignition problem stopped Coulthard from finishing third in his first Grand Prix at Barcelona, but for the balance of the season Williams decided to alternate Coulthard with former world champion Nigel Mansell. Coulthard responded by signing a deal with McLaren. Williams decided that it preferred to have Coulthard rather than Mansell, and so David became a full-time Williams driver in 1995. It was a year of learning, with some mistakes but also some impressive performances, culminating in his first victory at the Portuguese GP.

At the end of the year he left Williams to join Mika Hakkinen at McLaren. The two men were very evenly matched in 1996 but neither won a race, while in 1997 Coulthard topped the Finn in the world championship, winning in Australia and at Monza to score 36 points to Hakkinen's 27. But in 1998 Hakkinen was the man to beat, and although Coulthard won the San Marino GP it was his only victory of the year. Hakkinen won the world championship. It was a similar story in 1999, with David winning the British and Belgian GPs but being beaten to fourth place in the final title rankings.

In 2000 Coulthard won the British GP, and a week later was fortunate to emerge unscathed from a private jet crash at Lyons airport in which both pilots were killed. He bounced back quickly from this deeply unsettling experience to win again at Monaco, and in 2001 it was Coulthard rather than Hakkinen who led the McLaren attack against Michael Schumacher. Coulthard was again the lead driver for McLaren in 2002, although his new team-mate Kimi Raikkonen pushed him hard. Coulthard's victory at Monaco was, however, assured and brilliant, although in 2003 he was overshadowed by the Finn and McLaren announced that in 2005 it would be running Juan-Pablo Montoya. Coulthard moved to Red Bull Racing but he had a disappointing season in 2006. He was retained by the team for 2007 and will continue with them through 2008, which many believe will probably be his final season behind the wheel.

An even-tempered and amiable personality, Coulthard's biggest career handicap was his failure to gate-crash the close personal friendship which existed between McLaren boss Ron Dennis and Mika Hakkinen. The Scot always felt he was something of an outsider during his years at McLaren, although he showed great dignity handling the problem.

58. JO SIFFERT (Switzerland)

b. 7.7.1936, Fribourg, Switzerland; d. 24.10.1971, Brands
Hatch, England

*96 Grands Prix, 2 wins. Career span: 1962–63 (Lotus);
1964–65 (Brabham); 1966–67 (Cooper); 1968–69 (Lotus);
1970 (March); 1971 (BRM).*

Hugely underrated for much of his F1 career, Siffert's
first great day in the sun came one summer's afternoon
at Brands Hatch in 1968 when he steered Rob Walker's
Lotus 49B to a brilliant victory in the British Grand
Prix, just managing to keep a few feet ahead of the less
powerful but tenaciously driven Ferrari 312 of Chris
Amon all the way to the chequered flag.

Nicknamed 'Seppi' when he was a child, the young
Swiss would do anything to make money, from picking
and selling flowers to collecting spent Swiss army shells
which he would sell back to the thrifty services for
recycling. All this effort was focused on saving for a
motorbike and he duly started racing a 125cc Gilera in
1957, eventually winning the Swiss championship two
years later.

In 1960 he made the switch to four wheels in a Formula
Junior Stanguellini, and two years later he had found
his way into the sport's senior category, driving a Lotus 24
fitted with a 4-cylinder Climax engine. By 1965 he had
been swept into the delightfully paternalistic Walker team
family. And he twice beat Jim Clark to win the non-title
Mediterranean GP at Enna-Pergusa in Sicily in 1964 and
'65, also narrowly missing out on a similar success at
Siracusa in the latter season.

With the advent of the 3-litre F1 in 1966, Walker

slimmed down his entry to a single car, dropping Jo Bonnier from his driver line-up to concentrate solely on running Siffert. For 1968 Walker purchased one of the latest Lotus 49s, but the season almost ended in catastrophe even before it had started. Testing at a rain-drenched Brands Hatch prior to the Race of Champions, Siffert crashed heavily. The wreckage was returned to the team's base in Dorking where, as the car was being stripped down, a stray spark ignited a conflagration which not only destroyed the remains of the 49, but also reduced Rob's priceless ex-Dick Seaman ERA-Delage to ashes as well.

Thanks to the generosity of Rob's brother-in-law Sir Val Duncan, the team kept in business and a new Lotus was ordered in time for Siffert to deliver that memorable British GP success on the circuit where he'd made that near-disastrous slip early in the year. 'Seppi' stayed with Walker through to the end of 1969 before switching to the STP March squad, an arrangement which kept him away from Ferrari and still on the payroll of the JW Gulf Porsche team, available to contest all the classic endurance races.

In 1971 Siffert joined his old sports car racing rival Pedro Rodriguez in the BRM camp, but after the bold Mexican was killed in a sports car accident at the Norisring, the burden of team leadership fell onto 'Seppi's' broad shoulders. He coped magnificently, taking the BRM P160 to a commanding win in the Austrian GP. A great future beckoned, but fate stepped in and Siffert died in a fiery accident in the end-of-season non-championship race at Brands Hatch, scene of his greatest triumph.

57. PETER REVSON (USA)

b. 27.2.1939, New York; d. 22.3.1974, Kyalami, Johannesburg

30 Grands Prix, 2 wins. Career span: 1964 (Parnell Lotus); 1971 (Tyrrell); 1972–73 (McLaren); 1974 (Shadow).

Human nature being as it is, personal experience and exposure to an individual can be a defining factor in assessing that individual's talent. So it was for me in my professional capacity as the recently appointed Grand Prix correspondent of *Motoring News* during the latter half of the 1973 F1 championship season. McLaren driver Revson was extremely helpful and obliging to me as I was learning the sport's ropes, but I fancy he must have derived much amusement from a notably idiotic faux pas on my part while standing in the pit lane at Watkins Glen during the United States GP weekend.

Revson's striking girlfriend was understandably the centre of attention for photographers during the race weekend. I asked her what she did, and she replied that she was a model. Later that same day a colleague sidled up to me and asked whether I really was a complete idiot or just doing it for effect. 'That's Marjorie Wallace,' he hissed. I continued to look blank. 'She's Miss World,' he continued in exasperation. Not for nothing was Revson's autobiography called *Speed with Style* ...

A member of the Revlon cosmetics dynasty, this engaging American raced Formula Junior in Europe during the early 1960s, then briefly dabbled in F1 during 1964 with a Parnell team Lotus-BRM 24. Thereafter he concentrated on making his reputation in the USA before fortune brought him back to F1 with a two-year deal to drive for McLaren in 1972 and '73.

Quite a few people in the F1 community found Revson's cosmopolitan gloss a little tiresome, but if they harboured some reservations about his talent as a driver then Peter quickly put them straight. Armed with the splendidly competitive McLaren M23 he drove superbly to win the British GP at Silverstone, beating the hard-driven Ronnie Peterson's Lotus 72 into second place, with Denny Hulme in the other M23 and James Hunt in the Hesketh March 731. Later in the year he added another victory to his tally, this time in the Canadian GP at Mosport Park, only a few weeks before it was announced that he would be leaving McLaren at the end of the season to join the emergent Shadow F1 operation along-side Jean-Pierre Jarier.

Despite his success, Revson always had something of a strained relationship with the McLaren managing director Teddy Mayer, with whose late brother Timmy he had been a classmate at Cornell and later an F3 team-mate. Mayer wasn't always the easiest of guys to rub along with, but it was difficult to judge whether perhaps he resented Revson's success or the fact that the well-groomed New Yorker remained an uneasy link back to their heady days of youth. Whatever the reason, Revson wasn't staying at McLaren into '74 and, as a cheeky parting shot, offered the view that the Shadow DN3 was a better-handling car than the McLaren M23. Maybe so, but the DN3 would kill him after suffering a suspension failure during testing at Kyalami prior to the '74 South African GP.

56. LOUIS CHIRON (Monaco)

b. 1.8.1899, Monaco; d. 23.6.1979, Monaco

15 Grands Prix. Career span: 1950 (Maserati); 1951
(Maserati and Talbot); 1953 (Osca); 1955 (Lancia).

Tazio Nuvolari may claim the distinction of being the oldest GP winner, triumphing at Belgrade in 1939 when he was a little more than two months short of his 47th birthday, but it was the debonair Chiron who established the record of being the oldest participant in a round of the official world championship. He was a few weeks away from his 56th birthday when he drove a Lancia D50 into sixth place in the 1955 Monaco GP, 24 years after he had won the famous race at the wheel of a Bugatti.

Chiron's greatest days, arguably both on and off the track, came well before the war. An attractive man – his critics would say vain – his affair with Alice 'Baby' Hoffman, the wife of the Swiss industrialist Freddy Hoffman whose family ran the Hoffman LaRoche pharmaceutical empire, was the talk of the Grand Prix pit lanes throughout the 1930s. As a result, the Hoffmans' marriage collapsed, but Chiron proved so tardy in committing himself to his new lover that she eventually found solace in the arms of Rudi Caracciola, eventually becoming the famous German driver's second wife.

This clearly bothered Caracciola not in the slightest as, during the war, Chiron spent some time living with Rudi and 'Baby' in Lugano before marrying a Swiss girl. Despite being almost 50 by the time racing got seriously back into its swing after the war, Louis duly returned to the cockpit at the wheel of a Lago-Talbot, winning the

1947 and '49 French GPs as well as finishing second at Monaco in 1948.

By the time the official world championship was instigated in 1950, Chiron was well past his best, but he continued to compete intermittently as he wound down his international involvement, culminating in that outing at Monaco '55 which is better known for his Lancia team leader Alberto Ascari flying off the road into the harbour in a cloud of spume.

For many years thereafter Chiron acted as Clerk of the Course at Monaco, his lofty demeanour and snobbish manner being well in keeping with the race's snotty and aloof public image. He made great theatre – and usually chaos – of the whole starting procedure, allowing the cars to move forward from the dummy grid in ragged formation before dropping the starting flag and fleeing for his life, almost as if he resented the competitors of the day for being the centre of attention. Oh yes, and he memorably buttonholed Denny Hulme on his way to the 1967 rostrum ceremony by interjecting, 'And your name is, monsieur?'

55. CARLOS PACE (Brazil)

b. 6.10.1944, São Paolo, Brazil; d. 18.3.1977, nr São Paolo

72 Grands Prix, 1 win. Career span: 1972 (Williams); 1973–74 (Surtees); 1974–77 (Brabham).

Just as British race fans inevitably leap to the defence of Silverstone as an iconic cornerstone of the country's motorsporting bedrock, so Brazilian fans revere the

Autodromo José Carlos Pace at Interlagos, on the rundown fringes of Brazil's bustling second city.

The tarmac at Interlagos is where Brazilian motor racing legend has been writ large over the decades. Thirty-four years ago, a capacity crowd roared its hysterical approval as Emerson Fittipaldi, then the youngest world champion ever at 25, came storming into view to take the chequered flag and win his country's first Formula 1 world championship Grand Prix at the wheel of a slinky black-and-gold-liveried Lotus 72.

It was certainly the start of something big, with the man whose name the circuit now carries winning the race two years later at the wheel of one of Bernie Ecclestone's Brabhams and beating Fittipaldi, now at the wheel of a McLaren.

Pace has been gone now 30 years, killed in a light aircraft accident near São Paolo only weeks after finishing second in the 1977 Argentinian GP at Buenos Aires, but his memory is kept fresh by a bust alongside the main access road into the circuit paddock. Poignantly, it received a long overdue polish from one of the track workers on the Thursday afternoon before the 2007 championship clincher.

This debonair and charming Brazilian was a contemporary of the Fittipaldi brothers virtually from the start of his career, making his way to Britain in 1970 where he demonstrated great form at the wheel on an F3 Lotus 59. In 1971 he moved up to F2 with Frank Williams, winning a non-championship race at Imola, before gaining promotion into the Williams F1 team the following year, driving a March 711 as team-mate to Henri Pescarolo.

Despite having a long-term contract with Williams, Pace switched to Team Surtees for 1973, a move which seemed shrewd at the time but which collapsed amid contractual disagreement mid-way through 1974. He then joined the Bernie Ecclestone-owned Brabham team, alongside Argentinian Carlos Reutemann, for whom he scored that memorable '75 win at Interlagos, his only GP success.

Pace was suffused with optimism and enthusiasm when Ecclestone did a deal to use Alfa Romeo flat-12 engines from the start of '76, putting all his speed and commitment into getting the very best he could out of this new technical package. He opened the '77 season with a second place in the Argentine GP, an achievement which seemed to bode well for the rest of the season. Tragically, after only the first three races of the year, Pace was killed, leaving the Brabham team to mourn the passing of a true gentleman while quietly pondering just what he might have achieved had not fate intervened so cruelly.

54. JUAN-PABLO MONTOYA (Colombia)

b. 20.9.1975, Medellín, Colombia

92 Grands Prix, 7 wins. Career span: 2001–04 (Williams); 2005–06 (McLaren).

Here is another example of a potentially brilliant career which failed to deliver on its initial promise, largely because Montoya – basically an engaging and pleasant guy – demonstrated a destructive wilful independence which somehow prevented him from making the sort of compromises necessary to get the very best out of the various teams he worked for.

This was a man who should have won a world championship, but ended up falling out so badly with the management at McLaren in the summer of 2006 that he walked out of the team and turned his attention to NASCAR. Ever since his days driving in both CART and the Indy Racing League, Juan-Pablo had loved the US lifestyle and this, together with his preference for family life rather than the pressure-cooker intensity of the F1 business, shaped his future and dictated his priorities.

In 1997 he graduated to Formula 3000 with the RSM Marko team, winning three races and finishing second in the series to Ricardo Zonta. At the end of the year he was signed up as a test driver for the Williams team, agreeing to give the team first option on his services in F1 for five years. In 1998 he switched to the Super Nova team in Formula 3000 and won the title with four victories. He also completed 5,000 miles of testing with Williams.

With Williams recruiting Alex Zanardi and Ralf Schumacher for the 1999 season, there was no room for Montoya and so a deal was struck for him to race in America for two years to replace Zanardi in the Target Chip Ganassi Racing team. He took the championship by storm, winning the CART title at his first attempt with seven victories. The team then switched to Toyota power, and in the spring of 2000 Montoya gave Toyota its first CART victory in Milwaukee. The same year he competed in the Indianapolis 500 in a Ganassi-run IRL car and won the race at his first attempt. In 2001 he moved to Europe to be Ralf Schumacher's team-mate at Williams, and at the end of the year he won his first victory at Monza.

More frustration followed in 2002, with several pole positions but no victories, and Montoya went into 2003 hungry for sustained success. He should have won the championship that year but made a couple of costly mistakes and fell out with the team, signing for McLaren for 2005 before he had even started racing in 2004.

His move to McLaren in '05 was marked by missing two races after damaging a shoulder, and in the end he won three races and finished fourth in the world championship. Then came the falling-out with McLaren and the end of a less-than-perfect relationship, which said as much about the difficulties McLaren seemed to have when it came to driver management as it did Montoya's temperament.

53. JEAN ALESI (France)

b. 11.6.1964, Avignon

201 Grands Prix, 1 win. Career span: 1989–90 (Tyrrell); 1991–95 (Ferrari); 1996–97 (Benetton); 1998–99 (Sauber); 2000–01 (Prost).

There was always a child-like sense of unbridled enthusiasm radiated by this popular French driver throughout his F1 career, although it would be painfully fair to say that Alesi's level of achievement in the sport's most senior category fell well short of the promise he displayed on his way up the ladder to international stardom.

It was Jean's initially astonishing progress at the wheel of the taut and agile little Tyrrell-Cosworths in 1989 and '90 which sent several top team managers scurrying for their cheque books as they sought to get his name on a contract in time for the 1991 championship campaign. But although the cheerful little Frenchman had finished fourth on his GP debut at Paul Ricard in 1989, following this up with splendid second places at both Phoenix and Monaco the following year, these results proved far from the passport to instant success he'd been hoping for when he switched to the Ferrari team in 1991.

Of course, taking on the role of team-mate to Alain Prost was definitely calculated to put Alesi under considerable pressure from the start of his Maranello career, and the younger man did indeed have a difficult time. Yet while he did not quite display the out-and-out pace anticipated by some of his more over-optimistic fans, on several occasions he showed a strategic flair and shrewd tyre compound choice in potentially difficult conditions. Yet it would take Alesi until the 1995 Canadian GP in Montreal before he finally nailed his first GP success on his 31st birthday. As it transpired, it would be his only GP victory; and anyway his time at Ferrari would come to an end at the completion of the season, as Michael Schumacher had been signed to move from Benetton at the start of 1996.

Benetton boss Flavio Briatore was understandably less than delighted to have lost his protégé Schumacher to the famous Italian team, but signed Alesi together with Gerhard Berger for the '96 season, keeping his fingers firmly crossed that the title-winning momentum built up by the Benetton-Renaults the previous year would help keep the team in play. Unfortunately, things started off on an uncomfortable note with Jean unaccountably allowing his car to run out of fuel, having ignored increasingly agitated signals from the pit wall that he should come in and replenish his tank. This was almost too much for Briatore who, not mincing his words, pretty much told Alesi that he was an idiot. It was the moment when the Benetton boss got the message that neither Berger nor Alesi were quite in Schumacher's class. But, of course, very few were ...

After two years with Benetton, Alesi moved to Sauber, after which he rounded off his F1 career driving for the Prost-Peugeot squad. After fourteen seasons in F1 and only a single win to his credit, the time had come to bow off the GP stage for the popular Frenchman, who continued his links with the sport by competing successfully with the DTM Mercedes touring car team.

52. DENNY HULME (New Zealand)

b. 18.6.1937, Nelson, South Island, NZ; d. 4.10.1992, Bathurst, Australia

112 Grands Prix, 8 wins. World champion 1967. Career span: 1965–67 (Brabham); 1968–74 (McLaren).

Denny Hulme was one of the hardest of drivers to get to know if you were a journalist. He first spoke to me at the Nürburgring in 1973 and I remember very nearly jumping out of my skin with fright. His father Clive had won the Victoria Cross for his bravery during the Anzio landings during the Second World War, so in essence that was all you really needed to know about Denis Clive Hulme, variously 'Denny' or 'The Bear' to his acquaintances in the F1 pit lane, depending, I suppose, very largely on how you were getting on with him at any particular moment.

Yet if you chipped away at that granite edifice – and that certainly took time – then it was possible to discover a warm and generous personality lurking beneath the surface. But he was certainly a tough nut, reflecting the hard graft involved in climbing the ladder from lowly mechanic to Grand Prix winner, eventually rising to prominence in 1966 as Jack Brabham's team-mate in the Australian driver's team, a role into which he had gained promotion after Dan Gurney quit to establish his own Eagle squad at the end of 1965.

Jack won the championship – his third – in 1966, but Denny maintained the Brabham-Repco momentum the following year to snatch the title from his boss, possibly because Jack spent a lot of time toying with new and untried technical developments while Hulme used more proven and reliable machinery, much to his overall benefit. On the way to that title crown, Hulme won two Grands Prix. The first was at Monaco, scene of the tragic, fiery accident which cost the life of Lorenzo Bandini, the second at the Nürburgring, where he benefited from the mechanical frailty of the quicker Lotus 49 and Eagle Weslake.

In 1968 Hulme switched to drive for his old friend Bruce McLaren, remaining with this team until the end of his F1 driving career in 1974, although by then his fellow Kiwi star was long departed, killed in a testing accident at Goodwood in the summer of 1970. Bruce's loss utterly devastated Denny, for all his outward toughness, particularly as he himself was recovering from painful burns to his hands, caused by methanol leaking from an insecurely closed fuel filler cap on a USAC McLaren-Offenhauser while testing in preparation for the Indianapolis 500.

In 1973 he took the only pole position of his career on the debut outing of the striking McLaren M23 at Kyalami, and it was in one of these cars that he scored the final win of his F1 career, pressing home his advantage late in the chase in the '74 Argentine GP at Buenos Aires. He retired without fuss or fanfare at the end of that season, but later dabbled in touring cars, and it was in a BMW 3-series sedan that he apparently died at the wheel at the epic Mount Panorama track at Bathurst, Australia, just eighteen years later.

51. CLAY REGAZZONI (Switzerland)

b. 5.9.1939, Lugano; d. 11.12.2006, nr Parma

132 Grands Prix, 5 wins. Career span: 1970–72 (Ferrari); 1973 (BRM); 1974–76 (Ferrari); 1977 (Ensign); 1978 (Shadow); 1979 (Williams); 1980 (Ensign).

Gianclaudio 'Clay' Regazzoni, one of the iconic figures of Ferrari Formula 1 history, was killed in a car crash in Italy at the age of 67 during December 2006. The five-times Grand Prix winner, who twice triumphed at Monza driving for the Italian team, collided head-on with a truck on a main road near Parma while driving a Chrysler Voyager.

Niki Lauda, his team-mate at Ferrari from 1974 to 1976, paid tribute to a man whom he described as 'equalled only by James Hunt' in his ability to combine profession-alism behind the wheel with the extrovert, fun-loving image of the traditional racing driver. 'Clay was the sort of guy you could never forget,' said Lauda. 'He died as he lived, simply taking life as it came. He was a great blend of the professional and the playboy. He enjoyed life and was never negative.

'Even after the accident when he crashed his Ensign in the US GP West at Long Beach in 1980, a crash which left him paralysed from the waist down, he made the best out of his circumstances and was soon driving again in cars adapted with hand controls. When I joined Ferrari in '74 he was the star and I was the young kid, but I learned a great deal from him.' Regazzoni also won the hearts of British fans when he scored the Williams F1 team's maiden victory in the 1979 British Grand Prix at Silverstone, the last such success of the Swiss driver's career.

A rough, tough and uncompromising competitor from the Swiss canton of Ticino, Regazzoni was always something of a maverick. In the late 1960s, when the crusade for car and circuit safety was gaining momentum, Regazzoni was interested only in racing – and racing hard.

At that time, controversy was snapping at his heels. In 1968 he was implicated in the fatal accident involving the Englishman Chris Lambert's Brabham after a collision with Regazzoni's Tecno in the Dutch round of the European Formula 2 championship at Zandvoort. Regazzoni was subsequently exonerated.

In 1970 he returned to Zandvoort for his F1 debut at the wheel of a Ferrari, taking fourth place in a race marred by the death of the British driver Piers Courage, then two months later he scored a superb victory in the Italian Grand Prix after the world champion-elect Jochen Rindt was killed in practice.

He remained at Ferrari until the end of 1972, then moved to the British BRM squad for a barren season before returning to Ferrari for another three-year stint. In 1977 he drove for Ensign, in 1978 for Shadow, and then celebrated his 40th birthday with Williams before returning to Ensign where he ended his career the following year.

50. RICARDO RODRIGUEZ (Mexico)

b. 14.2.1942, Mexico City; d. 1.11.1962, Mexico City

5 Grands Prix. Career span: 1961–62 (Ferrari); 1962 (Lotus).

Ricardo Rodriguez was the younger of the two famous

Mexican motor racing brothers, and he stunned the Ferrari fans at Monza in 1961 by qualifying his Tipo 156 in second place on the grid for the Italian GP, only a fraction away from the pole position sister car driven by Wolfgang von Trips. He was nineteen years old, utterly confident in his own ability and sure in his belief that nobody – nothing – could touch him.

For the 1962 season Ricardo was a full-time member of the Ferrari F1 squad, but the team was now entering something of an uncompetitive trough, so the best he could manage was fourth at Spa-Francorchamps and sixth at Nürburgring. However, he did manage to sustain his morale by winning the Targa Florio, the epic no-holds-barred Sicilian road race, sharing a Dino 196SP with Willy Mairesse and Olivier Gendebien.

Ricardo clearly had a great career ahead of him, although at the time many people felt he was in the wrong environment at Ferrari, where young and in-experienced drivers too frequently found themselves under unacceptably intense pressure too early in their careers.

The young Mexican confessed that he was slightly irked when Ferrari declined to send a car to contest the first non-title Mexican GP at the end of the season, but fixed up a run in Rob Walker's Lotus 24 instead. Annoyed that John Surtees had posted a quicker lap than him – in a Lotus 24 borrowed from Jack Brabham – Ricardo overdid things as he attempted to redress the balance. The Lotus slammed over the lip of the banked Peraltada right-hander just before the startline, Rodriguez suffered multiple injuries and died shortly afterwards.

49. JACQUES VILLENEUVE (Canada)

b. 9.4.1971, Saint Jean Richelieu, Chambly, Quebec

162 Grands Prix, 11 wins. World champion 1997. Career span: 1996–98 (Williams); 1999–2003 (BAR); 2004 (Renault); 2005–06 (Sauber and BMW Sauber).

After many successes in America – becoming CART Champion, winning the Indianapolis 500 – Villeneuve came to F1 in 1996, with Williams-Renault. At Melbourne he became only the third driver to start his first Grand Prix from pole position, and only an engine problem kept him from winning the race.

At the end of that year, Patrick Head – the Williams technical director – considered the team's latest star. 'As a driver, he reminds me a little bit of Piquet, in that he's very, very, in control in the cockpit, as Nelson was. You'd be thinking, "Why isn't he going faster?" In fact, he was just doing his homework, working away – but then when it was time to go faster, he could just dive into it. I don't think Jacques gets flustered very easily.

'As a bloke, I think he's a bit of a one-off, really. Very self-contained. Maybe he needs Jock Clear, his race engineer, in his camp, but the impression he gives is that he doesn't really need the rest of us. It's almost as if he doesn't want to make any form of bond with the team – or with people generally, although he's got certain "insiders". You'd have to say he's very self-confident.'

Second to team-mate Damon Hill in the '96 world championship, Villeneuve went one better the following year, and in circumstances to make you believe maybe there is a God, after all. In the title-deciding race at Jerez, Michael Schumacher led, but Jacques reeled him in;

when he went for the lead, Schumacher tried to take him out. For once, happily, the biter was bitten back.

After three years with Williams, Villeneuve switched teams to join the BAR operation which had been established by his manager Craig Pollock with financial support from British American Tobacco, the intention being to construct a bespoke new F1 team around Villeneuve's personal ambitions. Perhaps predictably, the optimism which surrounded the upbeat launch of this new project was misplaced. The BAR squad struggled to make its mark and after four seasons Villeneuve stood down. He contested just three races for Renault at the end of 2004 before concluding a two-year deal with Sauber from the start of 2005.

This proved to be another disappointing association. BMW bought the team at the end of his first season driving for them, a development which added to the pressure felt by the 1997 world champion. Tensions began to simmer within the team and, after a succession of disappointing races, Jacques was suspended from the team after shunting heavily in practice for the 2006 German GP. This breach marked the end of the F1 road for the celebrated son of an arguably even more celebrated father.

48. JEAN BEHRA (France)

b. 16.2.1921, Nice; d. 1.8.1959, Avus, Berlin

52 Grands Prix. Career span: 1952–54 (Gordini); 1955, 1957–58 (Maserati); 1958 (BRM); 1959 (Ferrari).

Behra was an F1 lionheart who came to motor racing in

1950 after winning four French motorcycle championships on Moto Guzzi machines. His initial car outings came in a Maserati 4CLT and a 4.5-litre Lago Talbot, but it was not long before Amédée Gordini shrewdly selected him to join Maurice Trintignant, André Simon and Robert Manzon in his works team for the 1952 season.

The Simca-engined Gordinis were frail to a fault, however, and although Behra regularly flung himself into battle in heroic style, they were seldom rewarded with race finishes, let alone victories. Despite this, Behra was elevated to the status of French national hero in the summer of 1952, when his Gordini emerged triumphant in the non-championship Reims GP on a day when Alberto Ascari's pace-setting Ferrari wilted with mechanical trouble. At the time there was much uncharitable speculation to the effect that the Gordini had been running an oversize 2.5-litre engine on this occasion, but such unworthy thoughts were not allowed to intrude upon the joy of such a sun-soaked afternoon.

There was another such victory awaiting Behra in the 1954 Pau Grand Prix, where he beat Maurice Trintignant's Ferrari, and the same year saw him hanging on in the slipstream of the more powerful Mercedes W196s at Avus until his Gordini's sorely overtaxed engine eventually exploded. This performance brought him to the attention of the Mercedes team manager Alfred Neubauer, who toyed with the idea of signing Behra for 1955, but the Frenchman was already committed to Maserati and was about to enter the most satisfying phase of his F1 career with the seminal 250F.

The 1955 season saw him win non-championship F1 races at Pau and Bordeaux, and at Aintree his Maserati was the only interloper briefly to get in amongst the all-conquering Mercedes, although his season came to a near-disastrous end when he crashed heavily in the Tourist Trophy sports car race at Dundrod in Northern Ireland. He survived to recover, but with a false plastic ear to replace the one severed in this brutal crash.

In 1956 Behra accepted with characteristic dignity the reduced role of number two driver caused by the arrival of the brilliant Stirling Moss in the Maserati ranks, then, after a brief spell guesting for BRM, decided to join the Ferrari squad in 1959. Behra believed himself to be team leader, but rival Tony Brooks's winning pedigree soon asserted itself to add to the Frenchman's uncertainty and discomfiture.

On the 29th lap of the French GP at Reims, Behra's Ferrari Dino 246 rolled into the pits with a melted piston and its highly agitated driver became embroiled in a dispute which led to him punching team manager Romolo Tavoni. Behra was immediately fired and less than a month later died in a sports car race at Avus. The whole of France mourned, but there was not so much as a wreath at his funeral from the Ferrari team.

47. PEDRO RODRIGUEZ (Mexico)

b. 18.1.1940, Mexico City; d. 11.7.1971, Norisring circuit, Germany

55 Grands Prix, 2 wins. Career span: 1963 (Lotus);1964–65 (Ferrari); 1966 (Lotus); 1967 (Cooper); 1968 (BRM); 1969 (BRM and Ferrari); 1970–71 (BRM).

Along with his equally gifted brother Ricardo, Pedro Rodriguez raced motorcycles from his early teens and their wealthy father indulged them from an early age to the point where they had been behind the wheels of many high-performance cars well before reaching their 17th birthday.

Pedro was just twenty, two years older than his brother, when NART boss Luigi Chinetti brought them to Le Mans to share a Ferrari 250TR in 1960. The pair of them put the fear of God into the Maranello works team and might well have won, had their mount's hard-pressed V12 engine lasted the course. Ricardo's career was the more spectacular from the start, but the rising star was cut down brutally at the age of twenty when he crashed fatally battling for pole position at the '62 Mexican GP.

By contrast, Pedro's international reputation developed at a more measured pace. He got his first full-time F1 break with Cooper in 1967, lucking into a well-judged victory in that year's South African GP at Kyalami. He switched to BRM in 1968, lifting the battered team's morale in the wake of Mike Spence's death at Indianapolis with a succession of feisty drives, only to fall back into a part-time F1 role in 1969 when John Surtees took over as number one.

In 1970 Pedro's talent blossomed into full flower. He returned to lead the BRM squad, revelling in the power and poise of the fine-handling P153, behind the wheel of which he delivered a superbly disciplined victory in the Belgian GP. He had also assumed the crown as king of the sports car drivers, and his lurid antics at the wheel of the JW Gulf Porsche 917s further burnished his already glowing reputation as one of the sport's most accomplished professionals.

Rodriguez developed into a great Anglophile, living in Bray-on-Thames, driving a Bentley S1 and frequently to be photographed wearing a deerstalker. Yet in many ways the image he projected was an illusion; the relaxed life of an English country gentleman was not for him.

He wanted to race, race and race again. And with Jo Siffert as his team-mate it looked as though the BRM squad was poised for take-off after too long a spell in the doldrums.

Sadly, the week before the British Grand Prix, Pedro accepted an offer to drive Herbert Muller's Ferrari 512M in an inconsequential Interserie sports car race at the Norisring. Going like hell for the lead, he was edged into the wall lapping a slower car. The Ferrari erupted into flames and Pedro died shortly afterwards. It was the end of Mexico's great motor racing dynasty, and his departure left a huge void within the international motor racing community in which he had become one of the most popular personalities.

46. GERHARD BERGER (Austria)

b. 27.8.1959, Worgl, nr Innsbruck

210 Grands Prix, 10 wins. Career span: 1984 (ATS); 1985 (Arrows); 1986 (Benetton) 1987–89 and 1993–95 (Ferrari); 1990–92 (McLaren); 1996–97 (Benetton).

At the height of his racing achievement there was an underlying steel about Gerhard Berger's character which somehow belied his somewhat relaxed and easy-going outward nature. Blooded by three years in the highly political Ferrari F1 environment, he followed that facing the unenviable task of succeeding Alain Prost alongside Ayrton Senna in the second McLaren-Honda seat from the start of 1990.

It took the lanky Austrian the best part of two seasons to come to grips with the challenge, but towards the end of '91 he began to get on top of this very specific challenge and – at least in qualifying – started to hold his own against the dynamic Brazilian. It was as if Gerhard had at last got the final pieces of a complex jigsaw in place, a puzzle which it had seemed certain he would complete much earlier in his career, judging by his startling initial progress in the sport's premier league.

With F3 and touring car experience under his belt, this son of an Austrian road haulage contractor breezed into F1 at the wheel of an ATS-BMW towards the end of 1984. He obviously had the pace from the outset, accelerating quickly through a season with Arrows the following year and then on to join the Benetton-BMW squad, for whom he convincingly won the Mexican Grand Prix at the end of 1986.

By this time Gerhard had cut a deal to join Ferrari for 1987, winning the Japanese and Australian GPs in such style that it raised the prospect of his launching a challenge for the championship in '88. That proved to be a forlorn hope, as the rival McLaren-Hondas simply drove the opposition into the ground, although Berger picked up a lucky win at Monza after Senna and Prost both faltered. He had a rotten year in 1989 – now partnered by Nigel Mansell – and was supremely fortunate to escape with little more than superficial burns from a fiery, spectacular accident in the San Marino GP at Imola.

After his three seasons at McLaren he went back to Ferrari for another three-year stint before rounding off his career with two years at Benetton, driving superbly on his two final outings at Hockenheim in 1996 and '97. On the former occasion an engine failure caused his retirement in the closing stages, handing the win to Damon Hill's Williams, but in 1997 he scored his tenth and final GP win at the German track only weeks after his father had been killed in a light aircraft crash.

'At the end of the day there is nobody braver than Gerhard,' said Martin Brundle admiringly. And it certainly looked that way on this memorable Sunday afternoon. Gerhard was not away from the pit lane for long after retiring from the cockpit: first he had a stint as BMW's sporting director, and more recently returned as co-owner of Scuderia Toro Rosso with Red Bull boss Dietrich Mateschitz.

45. FRANÇOIS CEVERT (France)

b. 24.2.1944, Paris; d. 6.10.1973, Watkins Glen, USA

47 Grands Prix, 1 win. Career span: 1970–73 (Tyrrell).

François Cevert was a dazzlingly charismatic Parisian recruited in the summer of 1970 to partner Jackie Stewart in the Tyrrell-Ford squad, after his immediate predecessor Johnny Servoz-Gavin decided to quit the sport following an accident in practice for that year's Monaco GP. For the next three seasons Cevert loyally slipped into the role of Jackie's devoted pupil, maturing from strong number two to convincing front-line contender.

He won the 1971 US GP at Watkins Glen thanks to a combination of good luck and flawless driving, but by the summer of '73 his talent was close to its peak and Stewart acknowledged that the Frenchman was often genuinely quicker than he in some mid-season races – notably the Dutch and German GPs, in both of which they scored 1–2 finishes.

Cevert was being groomed to take over the Tyrrell team leadership in 1974 on Stewart's retirement at the end of the previous season, something the Scot had done a very good job of keeping from the rest of the F1 community. Yet hopes for a seamless transition were brutally dashed when François, pushing too hard in practice for the '73 US GP at Watkins Glen, crashed heavily at the high-speed uphill esses and was killed. The team withdrew from what had been supposed to be Jackie's final race, but the long-term consequences of Cevert's death denied Tyrrell the chance of maintaining its competitive momentum through the decades that followed.

'François was very, very good,' recalled Stewart to my journalistic colleague Maurice Hamilton of *The Observer*. 'In 1973 he was pacing himself against me. From April to October 1973 I knew I was not going to be participating again the following year, so there was no point in keeping anything from François, not that I did anyway. He was clearly going to be a major player in the future.

'Compared to today? Well, he wasn't Raikkonen, because he was no Ice Man. He wasn't Montoya, because he didn't have a Latin temperament and he was learning to drive a bit like Prost and like me, if you like. So, kind of Michael Schumacher, I suppose. Really, I had the highest respect for him. I think he probably would have won the 1974 world championship for Tyrrell.'

My personal memories of Cevert extend back to the Easter Monday F2 international at Thruxton in 1971, one of the major fixtures on the UK motor racing calendar. As a new *Motoring News* staff reporter I tentatively approached the Frenchman to ask if it would be possible to arrange an interview. François beamed; sure, it would be no problem.

In the lunch break between the two Saturday practice sessions he swept me up into his 6.3-litre Mercedes 300SEL, we tore into nearby Andover at breakneck speed, found a pub, had a cooked lunch and completed the interview. Then we rocketed back to the paddock at Thruxton where François continued practising in his Elf Tecno. By any standards he was a great guy.

44. GRAHAM HILL (Great Britain)

b. 15.2.1929, Hampstead, London; d. 29.11.1975, Arkley, nr London

176 Grands Prix, 14 wins. World champion 1962 and '68. Career span: 1958–59 (Lotus); 1960–66 (BRM); 1967–70 (Lotus); 1971–72 (Brabham); 1973–75 (Embassy Hill).

My most vivid memories of Graham Hill centre around two trips I took with him in his Piper Aztec, the aeroplane in which he and five others – including rising star Tony Brise – would eventually die when it crashed in fog on Arkley golf course one winter night in 1975. Cruising across Europe en route to an F2 race at Salzburgring with the plane on auto-pilot and Graham dozing quietly behind his sunglasses certainly seemed a laid-back way to behave to a novice like me. His death eventually came as a result of acute over-confidence – call it arrogance, if you like – and these were qualities which defined the man behind the public persona to a considerable extent.

The well-trimmed moustache and the saucy wink had helped Hill become one of the country's most identifiable sporting stars throughout the 'Swinging Sixties' at a time when his on-track reputation was at its zenith. Yet behind Graham's beaming public demeanour lurked a less charitable side to his character. Away from his adoring fans he could be crushingly rude and also singularly irresponsible – it emerged after his death that the plane was not properly insured. The bereaved families ended up having no option but to sue his estate for compensation.

It was a sad end to a career which had seen Graham's name in lights for much of the previous decade, even though for much of his racing career he spent his time very much in the shadow of his contemporary Jim Clark and his Lotus. Yet Hill was certainly a formidable competitor, spending most of the 1.5-litre F1 era running in Clark's wheel tracks. His gritty efforts also went a long way towards ensuring the survival of the BRM team – fast becoming a national joke until rescued by the Owen Organisation – and he memorably delivered them the world championship they had been craving for more than a decade at the end of the 1962 season. It was the beginning of a slow sunset on a great career.

He won Monaco five times – scoring a hat-trick for BRM in 1963–65 and then two more wins for Lotus in 1968–69. By then he had also won the '68 championship, steadying the Lotus team after the shattering experience of Clark's death at the start of that year, in much the same manner as his son Damon would do for Williams some 26 years later following the death of Ayrton Senna in the 1994 San Marino GP at Imola.

Finally, at the age of 40, Graham's luck ran out in the 1969 US GP at Watkins Glen. Limping back to the pits, seat harness undone, after a spin, a slow puncture finally deflated completely and he was thrown from the car in the ensuing accident. He suffered terrible leg injuries, but forced the pace of his recovery against the odds to score a point on his return at Kyalami the following year, now driving a private Lotus 49C for Rob Walker.

43. JEAN-PIERRE WIMILLE (France)

b. 26.2.1908, Paris; d. 28.1.1949, Buenos Aires

25 major race wins. Career span: 1932–37 (Bugatti); 1938 (Alfa Romeo); 1946–47 (Alfa Romeo).

Digging myself ever deeper into the mire of motor-sporting controversy, I realise that assessing Wimille's place in the history books is a more than usually difficult matter. Like Lang and Caracciola, there is no codified world championship points table from which it is possible to derive a firm starting point.

Yet there are some useful pointers. Fangio, who in many people's minds moved up to take Wimille's role as possibly the best driver of the immediate post-war generation, claimed he was inspired and motivated by the Frenchman. In fact this seemed to be very much a mutual admiration society. 'He'll be the one you are writing about one day,' said Wimille presciently of Fangio in 1947. That same year he also observed: 'put Fangio in a competitive car and he will surely do great things.' Both men were clearly close to the mark in their assessments, but only Fangio lived long enough to reap the rich harvest sown by his obvious racing talent.

Wimille, the son of a journalist, was just 22 when he made his racing debut in a Bugatti T37A, and he would become closely associated with the famous Italian marque which, in truth, was out of its depth commercially trying to compete consistently at the sport's most senior level. In 1937 Bugatti concentrated on sports car racing, and Wimille highlighted the season by winning at Le Mans. Then the company made a pretty feeble return to GP racing in 1938 before giving up mid-way through the programme, at which point Wimille was invited to join Alfa Romeo.

This was a strange situation, as the type 308 and 312 Alfas he raced were reportedly little better than the Bugattis – and he was not given a chance behind the wheel of one of the new 158s which would ultimately emerge as the dynamic force of the post-war period. Wimille at least had some consolation in winning Le Mans again for Bugatti, but then the war intervened and he played an active role in the Resistance after the fall of France.

After the war Wimille won the very first race to be held in France, when he triumphed in the memorial event in the Bois de Boulogne during September 1945. By the end of the following year he was back in the Alfa stable at the wheel of the 158 which had previously been denied him. In 1947 he had only two drives in this machine, winning both at Berne and Spa-Francorchamps, while in 1948 he posted a hat-trick of victories at Reims, Turin and Monza.

When not involved competing with Alfa Romeo, Wimille also had a deal to drive a little Formula 2 Gordini, one of which he took to South America for the winter series in 1947–48. While practising at Buenos Aires for the GP General Peron, he crashed into a trackside tree and succumbed to head injuries shortly afterwards.

42. JODY SCHECKTER (South Africa)

b. 29.1.1950, East London, South Africa

112 Grands Prix, 9 wins. World champion 1979. Career span:

1972–73 (McLaren); 1974–76 (Tyrrell); 1977–78 (Wolf); 1979–80 (Ferrari).

When he arrived in F1 as the McLaren team's raw and untutored rising star in 1972, Jody was quickly nicknamed 'Fletcher' after the baby seagull in the contemporary children's book Jonathan Livingstone Seagull who tried to fly at too early an age and kept crashing into the cliff face as a result.

From the outset 'Fletch' was undeniably world championship material, but he kept trying so hard that you really began to wonder whether or not the boy would survive long enough to make it. Single-handedly at Silverstone in 1973 he wiped out more than half the British GP field at the end of the opening lap. But he pulled everything together and really started to make his name as a serious contender with the Tyrrell squad the following year as Jackie Stewart's successor.

Jody originally exploded onto the British Formula Ford racing scene in 1971 driving a Merlyn Mk 11A which had previously been used by another astoundingly talented emergent star, Emerson Fittipaldi, to make his own reputation in the UK a couple of seasons earlier. There was just no question about it: Scheckter had intuitive skill literally flowing from his fingertips like high voltage static electricity. Yet it was also clear that he sometimes didn't have the judgement to temper his skill and, as he learned his profession, accidents featured quite prominently on his CV.

He spent three years with Tyrrell, then two driving for Walter Wolf's independent team. Finally at the start of 1979 he signed the two-year deal with Ferrari which would carry him to the world championship. Throughout that memorable '79 season he was partnered by the legendary Gilles Villeneuve, a driver with a very different personality than the South African, but a man with whom Jody bonded like a soulmate.

It also said much for Scheckter's rise to maturity that the way he handled the early races of the '79 season was both measured and intelligent. He may have been de facto number one driver in the Maranello squad, but anybody in that position might have felt pressured by the fact that Villeneuve scored the team's first two victories of the season. Yet Jody kept his cool and did not permit himself to become unduly flustered by the situation, correctly judging that while Gilles had the slight edge in terms of speed, the young Canadian was still prone to making slight driving errors bred from inexperience. Jody also knew he could totally depend on Villeneuve to abide by standing team orders and not try to overtake him as they ran in 1–2 formation throughout the championship clincher at Monza.

There was only one snag which caused tension between the two men. They both lived in Monaco and, when the call came for them to go to a Ferrari test at Fiorano, Scheckter's instinctive reaction was 'I'll drive'. The only thing scarier than driving with Gilles was flying there in his helicopter. And Jody didn't want to do that either.

41. GIUSEPPE FARINA (Italy)

b. 30.10.1906, Turin, Italy; d. 30.6.1966, nr Chambéry, France

33 Grands Prix, 5 wins. World champion 1950. Career span: 1950–51 (Alfa Romeo); 1952–55 (Ferrari).

Aloof and distant, Farina was something of a cold fish

who had few friends at the top level of motorsport. He never visited injured rivals in hospital, and throughout his own career, which was punctuated by accidents, he never expected them to afford him the compliment either. Back in the 1930s, collisions between Farina and both Marcel Lehoux (at Deauville) and Lazlo Hartmann (at Tripoli) had resulted in the deaths of both his rivals. He was also credited by many with having pioneered the relaxed, arms-stretched driving position later adopted by Stirling Moss.

Farina was a son of one of the founders of the Farina coachbuilding dynasty who qualified as a doctor of engineering and began his motor racing career at the wheel of a 1.5-litre Alfa Romeo in the 1932 Aosta–Grand St Bernard hill-climb event. It was perhaps not the most memorable of competition debuts – he crashed heavily, sustaining a broken shoulder and facial lacerations.

By the end of 1934 Farina was racing a Maserati 4 CM, winning the Circuit of Biella, and then taking his first major victory in the voiturette race which acted as a curtain-raiser for the Czech GP at Brno. He continued campaigning in another Maserati the following year, before being recruited to drive for the Scuderia Ferrari, a crucial move which brought him in contact with the great car which would carry him to international fame and good fortune.

He raced the legendary Alfa 158s under the Scuderia Ferrari banner before the war, and it was at the wheel of one of these straight-eight 1.5-litre supercharged monsters that he clinched the first official world championship in 1950 with wins in the British, Swiss and Italian GPs. After this title success Farina's career dropped away steadily through to his retirement at the end of the 1955 season, during which he competed in only a handful of races, the lingering acute discomfort from burns suffered at Monza the previous year only partly allayed by pain-killing drugs. Away from F1 he mounted a couple of half-hearted attempts at the Indy 500 in 1956 and '57 and, in his retirement, briefly imported Jaguar cars to Italy before becoming an Alfa Romeo main agent.

Farina was driving a Lotus-Cortina on his way to the 1966 French GP when he crashed fatally into two telegraph poles after being caught out on a slippery road surface in the mountains near Chambéry just a few months short of his 60th birthday.

40. MIKE HAWTHORN (Great Britain)

b. 10.4.1929, Mexborough, Yorkshire, England; d. 22.1.1959, Guildford bypass

45 Grands Prix, 3 wins. World champion 1958. Career span: 1952 (Cooper); 1953–54 (Ferrari); 1955 (Vanwall and Ferrari); 1956 (BRM, Maserati and Vanwall); 1957–58 (Ferrari).

Almost 50 years have passed since the death of Britain's first F1 world champion in a road accident only a few months after announcing his retirement from driving, and there are still a few of his contemporaries alive who will testify to Mike's gregarious character and talent behind the wheel.

Yet the more I hear about Hawthorn the more I'm forced to conclude that he was really a bit of a pain. OK, so he lived in different times when boozing and carousing were all part of the F1 driver's repertoire, but if one flips through his memoirs, *Challenge Me the Race* and *Champion Year,* he comes across as a tiresomely self-indulgent character wedded to his own small coterie of close friends.

Truth be told, he was a pretty inconsistent F1 driver, good on his day but not in the same class as Vanwall team-mates Stirling Moss and Tony Brooks, both of whom he beat to the title crown. That said, Hawthorn certainly caught the public's imagination with his wheel-to-wheel between his Ferrari and Juan-Manuel Fangio's Maserati for victory in the 1953 French GP at Reims.

Hawthorn was also unfortunate in being hounded by the sensational end of the British daily newspaper market, being accused of dodging his national service, and this matter concerning one of England's most high-profile sportsmen even prompted discussions in the House of Commons. In truth, Mike suffered from a kidney ailment which would almost certainly have rendered him ineligible, but the fact remained that a broad swathe of public opinion could not reconcile this reality with the fact that he was fit enough to race F1 cars.

Hawthorn might well have been excluded from winning the 1958 title crown had his rival Stirling Moss not stood up for him after the Ferrari driver spun in the Portuguese GP and was apparently pushed against the direction of traffic by marshals trying to get him back in the race. It seemed as though he indeed might well be excluded, but Moss spoke up to say that his rival's Ferrari was in fact on the pavement at the time and therefore there was no penalty to be considered. The stewards accepted Moss's word, so Mike was permitted to keep his position.

Moss was poorly paid back for his sportsmanship by Ferrari. In the final race of the year at Casablanca, Phil Hill was instructed to relinquish his second place to a recovering Hawthorn during the closing stages in order to secure Mike's championship. It was just the sort of behaviour which would come back to haunt Ferrari again and again more than 40 years later as Michael Schumacher took F1 – and his team-mates – by the throat and gave the sport a good mauling.

39. DAMON HILL (Great Britain)

b. 17.9.1960, Hampstead, London

115 Grands Prix, 22 wins. World champion 1996. Career span: 1993–96 (Williams); 1997 (Arrows); 1998–99 (Jordan).

Damon Hill's most impressive race came in the pouring rain at Suzuka in 1994 when he out-foxed Michael Schumacher on a near-flooded circuit to win the Japanese Grand Prix in truly superb style. It was yet another example of how the serious-minded Londoner could raise the level of his game when the pressure was really on.

Hill's advancement through the F1 ranks was certainly fortunate, but he superbly capitalised on any opportunity which came his way. A test driving role with the Williams squad led to promotion to a race seat alongside Alain Prost in 1993 after Nigel Mansell decided he would pursue a career on the US Champcar scene. In 1994 he picked up the baton for Williams after Ayrton Senna's death, lost his chance of the title after Schumacher helped him off the road in Adelaide, but two years later finally took the championship.

It was the controversy in Adelaide which really served to put Hill on the international map as a major sporting personality. Initially his front-line F1 career had been played out with him taking an essentially junior role alongside the two superstars of their era. But with Senna's death bruising the Williams psyche deeply, in a sense it was left for Damon to pick up the pieces and provide the bedrock on which to rebuild the team's morale and self-respect. He became known not simply for being the son of the late Graham Hill, the twice world champion from the 1960s, but could now stand tall as a winner in his own right. The transition was as powerful as it was all-pervading.

Although he subsequently raced for Arrows and Jordan, it will be for his four years at Williams that Damon will best be remembered. He was not to be stopped in 1996. He started the year with three straight wins at Melbourne, Interlagos and Buenos Aires, after which his Williams FW18 stormed to further victories at Imola, Montreal, Magny-Cours, Hockenheim and in the season finale at Suzuka. In the process Damon had fought off a mounting challenge from Villeneuve which went all the way to the final race.

So what was his reward? A lucrative new contract for 1997? A generous multi-million dollar success bonus? No, none of those things. Damon's reward for those efforts was to be dropped from the team by Frank Williams. F1 can certainly sometimes be a funny old world.

After Williams he enjoyed a season with Arrows, then two years with the Jordan squad, highlight of which was a beautifully driven performance to win the saturated 1998 Belgian GP at Spa-Francorchamps, a performance which very nearly matched his win at Suzuka four years earlier for sheer class and conviction.

38. PHIL HILL (USA)

b. 20.4.1927, Miami, Florida

48 Grands Prix, 3 wins. World champion 1961. Career span: 1958–62 (Ferrari); 1963 (ATS); 1964 (Cooper); 1965 (Centro Sud).

Many people shared the view that this pleasant Californian was simply too intelligent to be a racing driver, let alone to work for Enzo Ferrari at a time when the Italian team boss was at the absolute peak of his cantankerous powers. Although born in Florida, Phil was brought up in Santa Monica, a genteel, leafy enclave of Los Angeles suburbia fronting onto the Pacific Ocean.

One of only two Americans to take the crown, he secured the 1961 title with victory in Ferrari's home race which was tragically marred by the death of his team-mate Wolfgang von Trips and fourteen spectators when the German count's car flew into the crowd after colliding with Jim Clark's Lotus.

It had been a fraught season for Hill in his role as de facto Ferrari team leader and the most seasoned F1 driver in the team, which also included his fellow American Richie Ginther. Ferrari for the most part let his men fight among themselves, his 'survival of the fittest' strategy being designed to let the quickest man assert himself on any particular day. On the face of it, this might have seemed to be a fair and democratic way to behave. Yet, in truth, the Commendatore was only on distant nodding acquaintance with both words.

Phil stayed with Ferrari through 1962, to be totally eclipsed by the new breed of British V8 challenger from

BRM and Coventry-Climax, then made a disastrous career move to the fledgling ATS team which had been established by a breakaway group of Ferrari renegades. It almost torpedoed his career for good, but salvation seemed to be at hand with the offer of a drive for Cooper alongside Bruce McLaren. But nothing went right with this relationship either.

When Phil wrote off two cars in the '64 Austrian GP meeting on the Zeltweg aerodrome, a frustrated John Cooper suspended him. Although reinstated in the team for the last couple of races, Phil knew he was approaching the twilight of his career, and some drives in a second-hand Centro Sud BRM heightened that realisation the following year.

Hill's F1 career continued in a gentle decline until the end of 1965, but he continued racing sports cars for another two years, rounding off his 1967 season with a fine victory in the BOAC 1000KM endurance event, sharing the distinctive winged Chaparral with Britain's Mike Spence.

At the start of the following year, the quiet and introspective gentleman suddenly remembered that he had forgotten to renew his international competition licence and, in his own words, 'found that I had become a retired racing driver'.

This did not worry him at all. He withdrew to Santa Monica to concentrate on his thriving old car restoration business, as well as being a regular attendee of historic car gatherings throughout the world. Even slowed by the onset of illness as he approached 80, he could still turn a mean lap or two around Goodwood in a Ferrari 'Testa Rossa' in 2006.

37. JAMES HUNT (Great Britain)

b. 29.8. 1947, Belmont, Surrey; d. 15.6.1993,
Wimbledon, England

*92 Grands Prix, 10 wins. World champion 1976. Career span:
1973–75 (Hesketh); 1976–78 (McLaren); 1979 (Wolf).*

Niki Lauda, the man who raced wheel-to-wheel against
Hunt for the '76 world championship, has the most
succinct and touching memories of the man with whom
he grew to F1 competitive maturity. 'What you've got to
understand about my relationship with James is that it was
based on a lot of mutual respect built up over the four
years,' said Niki reflectively. 'I'd first met him in 1971
when I'd come to England to drive for the semi-works
March F2 team. I really didn't know too many people and
I rented a studio flat from Max Mosley just around the
back of Victoria Station.

'Ronnie Peterson was my team-mate at the time and
he sort-of knew James, who at that time was doing a lot
of crashing in one of the March Formula 3 cars. But it
was the connection with March that really enabled me to
get to know James. He lived in Fulham, as I recall,
and despite the fact we were pretty directly opposed
competitors, we knocked around a lot together socially
and became good friends.

'The truth of it was that I think we were both rebels to
some extent. Our friendship was definitely strengthened
by the fact that both our families were pretty seriously
opposed to our being involved in motor racing. James's
parents had told him pretty directly that they weren't
prepared to fund his motor racing. But at least he didn't
have a grandfather telephoning his potential sponsors

telling them not to get involved with them, which was something that happened to me early on in my racing career.

'It was also fairly clear that, while I tended to be portrayed as the serious one among the group, beneath all that "Hunt the Shunt" image – which was nonsense, in my view – I quickly formed the view that James would be one of the guys I'd have to beat if and when we ever made our way up into Fl.'

Hunt was one of those rare talents who successfully turned around an early career which seemed to be going nowhere but the scrap heap. In 1972 he was known for precious little apart from wrecking racing cars; a year later he'd finished fourth in the British GP at Silverstone driving Lord Hesketh's March. Two years further along he was winning the Dutch GP at Zandvoort in his Lordship's home-brewed racer, the Hesketh 308, and then it was onwards and upwards to 1976 world championship glory at the wheel of the McLaren vacated at the end of the previous season by twice title-holder Emerson Fittipaldi. His career gradually petered out towards the end of the decade.

Off track, James would become an ever-present item in the gossip columns, never more than when his first wife Susy went off with acting legend Richard Burton. He made quite a success for himself of BBC television commentaries alongside Murray Walker, but it was only after his death from a heart attack in the summer of 1993 that his friends realised just what a battle with depression he had waged during the last few years of his life.

36. ALAN JONES (Australia)

b. 2.11.1946, Melbourne

116 Grands Prix, 12 wins. World champion 1980. Career span: 1975 (Hesketh and Hill); 1976 (Surtees); 1977 (Shadow); 1978–81 (Williams); 1983 (Arrows); 1985–86 (Lola).

Alan Jones was admittedly an unlikely champion. His great days with Williams were somehow book-ended and shaded by Mario Andretti's high-profile championship for Lotus in '78 and the emergence of Alain Prost in the early 1980s. But let's be clear what we mean. It wasn't his talent and guts at the wheel over which there was any question. Once he established a foothold in the F1 business he unquestionably delivered. Yet in the junior formulae during the 1970s his star had never quite shone as brightly as those of Roger Williamson, Tom Pryce or Tony Brise. Ironically, he would outlive all three and get his big chance as a result of Pryce's tragic death in the 1977 South African GP at Kyalami.

Jones made that once-in-a-lifetime opportunity work for him. Wringing everything he could from the heavy Shadow DN8, Alan was in the right place at the right time when James Hunt's McLaren M26 suffered an engine failure at the Osterreichring. Victory in the Austrian GP fell into Alan's lap. He was on his way, having seized the moment, and now looked so obviously a coming man that it was surprising that more people were not jostling for his services at this moment in time.

One of the men who was watching was Frank Williams. Frank was busy re-establishing himself in the F1 business after selling the remnants of his original company to the

Austro-Canadian oil magnate Walter Wolf. Now he was looking for a driver.

'Hans Stuck, Gunnar Nilsson and Alan were on our list,' recalled Frank. 'All I can say is that if you work backwards over the years, you can see we've made all sorts of bum driver selections, but Jones was a great one.'

Alan's father Stan had been hugely inspirational in shaping his son's ambitions. Stan Jones was a famously hard-driving, hard-living competitor from another era who ensured that Alan's enthusiasm for the sport was fired at an early age. When his father raced Maseratis and Coopers 'down under' in the 1950s the short-trousered Alan can be seen in most of the photographs. It was a long hard slog for him to gain success when he came to Europe, but he inherited his father's grit and determination, which certainly stood him in good stead over a distinguished F1 career.

At the end of 1981 Jones retired from F1, ostensibly to look after his farm and other business interests back in Australia. But by 1983 he was getting restless and duly reappeared driving an Arrows in the US GP at Long Beach. It didn't lead to anything, but two years later he received a tempting financial offer to return again with the emergent Haas Lola squad. It turned out to be a disaster. The glory days with Williams were gone for good.

35. JACKY ICKX (Belgium)

b. 1.1.1945, Brussels

116 Grands Prix, 8 wins. Career span: 1967 (Cooper); 1968 (Ferrari); 1969 (Brabham); 1970–73 (Ferrari); 1974–75

(Lotus); 1976 (Williams and Ensign); 1977–78 (Ensign); 1979 (Ligier).

Jacky Ickx's early motor racing achievements marked him out as a potential world champion even before he first sat in the cockpit of an F1 car. Yet somehow the cards never fell in the direction of this articulate and civilised Belgian driver, despite some quite brilliant drives for Ferrari and Brabham between 1968 and '72.

Ickx scored a championship point at Monza in 1967 at the wheel of a Cooper-Maserati, but it was his success in winning the close-fought European F2 championship in a Tyrrell team Matra MS7 which really marked him down as something special. He drove this car so superbly in the F2 class of that year's German GP at the Nürburgring that Jackie Stewart – contesting the same race in the ponderous and scarcely more powerful BRM H-16 – actually suggested to Tyrrell after his own retirement that Ickx should be slowed down in the interests of his own self-preservation. Ken declined the invitation.

For 1968 he switched to Ferrari, driving brilliantly to win the rain-soaked French GP at Rouen-les-Essarts, and was in the running for the world championship right up to the Canadian GP where a stuck throttle in practice resulted in a broken leg. For 1969 he moved to the rival Brabham squad, a move engineered by the Gulf Oil Corporation who wanted Ickx to drive their GT40 sports cars – a worthwhile exercise, as Jacky and his co-driver Jackie Oliver won the closest Le Mans victory in years.

The 1970 season saw Ickx return to Ferrari, where he used the superb new flat-12 312 to win the Austrian, Canadian and Mexican GPs, only just failing to exceed the points total accumulated by Jochen Rindt prior to his death at Monza. Disappointingly, the '71 season yielded little for Ickx, but 1972 saw him win the German GP at Nürburgring for the second time in his career. Apart from a great win in the sodden '74 Brands Hatch Race of Champions in a Lotus 72, there would be no more F1 success awaiting Ickx, although he raced through to 1979 before quitting the sport's senior category.

Ickx subsequently became clerk of the course for the Monaco GP, but had his licence withdrawn in outrageous circumstances following the 1984 race when he was obliquely accused of favouring Alain Prost's Porsche-engined McLaren, which had just emerged victorious after he flagged the race to a premature halt in monsoon conditions. Ickx's links with Porsche, said the critics, made him partial, presumably on the basis that he had driven the German cars successfully in a wide variety of international sports car races.

This in fact was a ludicrous reflection on the governing body's inability to rule the sport in an even-handed manner. Gentlemen who knew their stuff, like Ickx, were rare gems and badly needed on the administrative side of the sport. Happily – and mercifully – Ickx emerged with his reputation intact and undamaged.

34. DIDIER PIRONI (France)

b. 26.3.1952, Paris; d. 23.8.1987, off Isle of Wight, England

70 Grands Prix, 3 wins. Career span: 1978–79 (Tyrrell); 1980 (Ligier); 1981–82 (Ferrari).

A dour and focused personality, Pironi was driven by a

burning desire to become France's first official world champion, an ambition he very nearly achieved in 1982. He was something of a cold fish, a man who always seemed to have his emotions and temperament reined in and under firm control. After his team-mate Gilles Villeneuve was killed practising for the '82 Belgian GP at Zolder, it looked as though the title was there for the taking.

Sadly, Pironi's own title hopes came to an end when he was involved in a massive accident practising for that year's German GP at Hockenheim. In ominous conditions of heavy rain and mist, his Ferrari vaulted over a rear wheel of Alain Prost's Renault, leaving Didier with serious leg injuries which ended his racing career.

Inspired by the racing exploits of his cousin, the late José Dolhem, Pironi steadily climbed through the French motor racing infrastructure, winning the prestigious Monaco GP supporting race in 1977, after which his achievements attracted the close scrutiny of Ken Tyrrell who signed him for the '78 season as team-mate to Patrick Depailler. He duly signalled his potential by scoring championship points in four of the first six races, added to which he scored a great win at Le Mans for the Renault turbo team. In fact the French national team wanted him to race for them in F1, but Tyrrell held him to his contract and Pironi spent a second year driving for Ken's team before switching to Ligier in 1980.

For Ligier he won the Belgian GP at Zolder in fine style, seeing off Alan Jones's Williams FW07 in the process, and led Jones again at Monaco. In 1981 when he joined Ferrari he was clearly outclassed by Gilles Villeneuve, whom he psychologically destabilised by beating him in the '82 San Marino GP at Imola against team orders. The supposed friendship between the two men was now at an end; the traffic rift was never resolved, as Villeneuve was killed while practising for the following race at Zolder.

Pironi went on to win the Dutch GP in masterly style before that terrible accident at Hockenheim cut short his season. All that lay ahead of him now were dozens of painful operations over the years to repair his damaged legs, as predictions about a possible return to the F1 cockpit seemed ever more speculative and optimistic.

Yet Pironi remained restless for a sporting challenge, instead turning his hand to the equally dangerous and spectacular sport of powerboat racing. Off Cowes in the Solent, he ran flat-out through the churning wake of a passing oil tanker without easing back the throttles. The powerboat flipped over, killing Pironi and his two crew members, journalist Bernard Giroux and the former F3 racer Jean-Claude Guenard.

33. RUDOLF CARACCIOLA (Germany)

b. 30.1.1901, Remagen, Germany; d. 28.9.1959, Lugano, Switzerland

52 Grands Prix, 16 wins. Career span: 1932–33 (Alfa Romeo); 1934–39 (Mercedes-Benz).

One of the great heroes of the pre-war European racing scene, Rudolf Caracciola was the most successful member of the Mercedes factory team from 1934 to '39, winning the European championship crown – effectively the forerunner of the world championship – in 1935, '37 and '38.

Caracciola had contested only minor league races in the mid-1920s, which led to a job with Mercedes, although initially only as a salesman. He later raced their formidable SSK sports cars, dominating the 1931 Mille Miglia to become the first non-Italian to win that epic road race. In 1932 Caracciola drove for Alfa Romeo and then established his own private team for the following year together with Frenchman Louis Chiron, both driving ex-works Alfas. Unfortunately Caracciola crashed badly in practice for Monaco and did not race again for more than a year, as he battled to recover from a shattered hip which would leave him with one leg shorter than the other for the rest of his life.

He duly returned to Mercedes in 1934 and by the time the Second World War rang down the curtain on this epic era in 1939 he had won sixteen races out of 52 starts, a 30.8 per cent success rate, which was exceeded during that period only by the legendary Bernd Rosemeyer who won ten races from 33 starts.

Sadly, Caracciola attempted to restart his career after the war years, but the spark had gone out. Like Lang, he was not the driver he had been back at the end of the 1930s. Perhaps foolishly, he tried his hand on the Indianapolis oval in 1946, his mind set on participating in the Indy 500, but he crashed heavily. Thereafter Rudi was a mere shadow of his former self, walking unsteadily and wobbly on his feet; yet still he would not give up. Mercedes team manager Alfred Neubauer touchingly gave him the chance to race one of the pre-war W163s in Argentina during 1951. Caracciola was no fool, declining the invitation as the cars were clearly far too old. But he finished fourth in the 1952 Mille Miglia driving one of the new 300SL coupes, and also intended to contest Le Mans. Unfortunately he crashed heavily at Berne a few weeks before Le Mans, again sustaining serious leg injuries. This time there was to be no comeback and he died before even reaching his 60th birthday.

'Caracciola was the best driver I ever competed

against,' said his former team-mate Manfred von Brauchitsch more than 50 years later. 'He was good and fair, a very convivial fellow. We had a good relationship for many years, both on and off the circuit. We were slightly older than most of the others and formed a deep personal bond.'

32. FERNANDO ALONSO (Spain)

b. 29.7.1981, Oviedo, Spain

102 Grands Prix, 19 wins. World champion 2005 and '06. Career span: 2001 (Minardi); 2003–06 (Renault); 2007 (McLaren).

It seems like only yesterday that he was the bubbly, fluffy young Spanish kid from Oviedo hanging around the Renault F1 team kitchens in 2002, helping the chef make pizzas on Friday afternoons. Then he was the team's test and reserve driver, twiddling his thumbs, frustrated at being on the sidelines.

Just a year had passed since he'd caught our attention in the Monaco media centre. An in-car cockpit shot of a Minardi popped up on the screen. The driver's hands were an unimaginable blur as he shaved the barriers with meticulous precision. Who the hell is this, we wondered? It was Fernando, his 20th birthday still two months away, laying down a marker for the future.

'For me, dealing with Fernando is like watching a movie for the second time,' said Renault team boss Flavio Briatore, highlighting the similarity to his other protégé Michael Schumacher. 'No problem. Every time you see a movie you've seen before, you keep being reminded of little bits which caught your attention first time around.'

Pat Symonds, Renault's executive director of engineering, adds another perspective. 'The real similarity I see between the two is their self-belief,' he said. 'Like Michael, Fernando has total conviction in his own abilities – he is able to see the target he has to reach, and to then go out and achieve it.

'It is almost as if these guys set a personal best every time they get in the car. I think it is characteristic of champions – and although I cannot prove it, I could almost guarantee that it would be the same in other sports – that ability to perform when it counts.' Small wonder that Alonso became the youngest F1 world champion of all time in 2005 and then repeated the achievement the following year.

Yet by the end of the 2007 season, after a single year with McLaren, Alonso's image had been terminally blighted and his reputation as possibly the most complete performer in F1 lay in ruins.

Whether he was driven by paranoia or a genuine belief that McLaren had promised him a performance advantage that it failed to deliver is difficult to say. If it was the former, it was probably the result of listening to whispers from his tight-knit coterie of Spanish insiders. If the latter, he must stand guilty of never having probed McLaren's long-established tradition of trying to ensure complete equality of opportunity between both its drivers at all times.

This hugely talented driver therefore found himself facing the task of rebuilding his battered reputation in 2008, a year which promised to be far more demanding for him than anything that had gone before.

31. NIGEL MANSELL (Great Britain)

b. 8.8.1953, Upton upon Severn, England

187 Grands Prix, 31 wins. World champion 1992. Career span: 1980–84 (Lotus); 1986–88 (Williams); 1989–90 (Ferrari); 1991–92 (Williams); 1994 (Williams) 1995 (McLaren).

Nigel Mansell was certainly a tough customer. A teenage karting star, he'd never quite mustered sufficient backing to break into the big time as he battled up through the junior formulae. His big break came in 1980 when Colin Chapman, the charismatic Lotus boss, offered him a chance of a test drive at the Paul Ricard circuit in southern France. He made his F1 debut in the Austrian GP that year, sitting in a bath of petrol for much of the race distance after his Lotus 81's fuel tank sprang a leak. He suffered in silence and the reward for his resilience came the following year when he was recruited to drive full-time for the team alongside the Italian Elio de Angelis.

The qualities in Mansell which persuaded Williams to give him a chance in 1985 were forged during those four problematical years with Lotus. Chapman had seen past Nigel's chippy and argumentative exterior and identified that this bullishly confident young man had a genuine talent. He also had the speed necessary to get the job done, but by the time his tenure with Lotus had come to an end, one was bound to wonder whether he had sufficient good luck to be a worthwhile bet.

Mansell spent three years with Williams, then switched to Ferrari for two years, decided to retire, changed his mind, returned to Frank's team to win the '92 title, fell

James Hunt was one of the most colourful personalities ever to contest the F1 world championship, but ultimately he probably wasn't as good as his close pal Niki Lauda. The 1976 world champion ranks 37th, some seventeen places behind his Austrian rival.

Jackie Stewart claims eighth place in this top 100. Not simply because the author is a fan, and counts himself a friend of the gregarious Scot, but because he won his third world championship in 1973 at the wheel of a car which was even more difficult to drive than he coyly acknowledges. The trademark Beatles thatch has yet to appear in this short-back-and-sides photograph.

Third in these rankings, and perhaps laying claim to an even higher placing had it not been for his tempestuous mood swings, the late Ayrton Senna had the touch of unbridled genius which helped him steer a path to three world championships.

Jenson Button may have only a single Grand Prix victory to his credit at the time of completing this volume, but he has displayed such rounded talent and resilience as to make his 67th place ranking look conservative in the minds of many observers.

Kimi Raikkonen gains 29th place in these rankings, just one place behind fellow Finnish world champion Keke Rosberg, after snatching the 2007 title crown with victory in the final race of the season at Interlagos.

Mario Andretti won the 1978 world championship brilliantly for Lotus, adding lashings of personal charisma to a rounded talent which also saw him win the 1969 Indianapolis 500 as well as a host of sports car races all over the world. He claims a well-merited 19th overall in these rankings.

Chris Amon took 13th place in these rankings, despite never having won a Grand Prix. Have we gone mad? Not one bit of it. Jackie Stewart rates the mild-mannered New Zealander as one of the very best drivers he ever raced against.

Had that great Anglophile Pedro Rodriguez lived beyond the summer of 1971 he would almost certainly have boosted his tally of Grand Prix victories beyond the meagre two wins he'd scored up to that point. He squeezes inside my top 50, claiming 47th position in the final rankings.

Emerson Fittipaldi won F1 world championships for Lotus (1972) and McLaren (1974) before making his home in the USA, where he added a couple of Indy 500 victories to his glowing CV. A truly great driver, he earns 17th place in our ratings.

Fated Ferrari duo: you can sense the tension in this shot of 1982 Maranello team-mates Didier Pironi (left, 34th place) and his colleague Gilles Villeneuve (12th).

Dan Gurney checks in at 27th, rated by the late Jim Clark as one of the handful of truly great drivers that the Scot found extremely difficult to beat.

Lewis Hamilton's 30th place ranking reflects what he might do in the future as much as his dazzling McLaren debut in 2007. Come back in three years and he'll likely be a top ten contender.

Jack Brabham was a tough and resilient operator who remains the only man to win a world championship in a car bearing his own name, in 1966. I reckon 18th place pretty much reflects his enduring status in the motor racing community.

out with him and left again, went to race CART, returned
to F1 with Williams in 1994, then switched to McLaren in
'95 only to leave the team after a handful of races.

Mansell's supporters may well be displeased to see their
man rated only 31st in this very personal ranking of the
top 100 Grand Prix drivers of all time. Yet for all his
genius, I would contend that there are few drivers who
have won world championships equipped with cars which
afforded such a performance edge as Nigel enjoyed with
the Williams FW14B in 1992.

If this is interpreted as a criticism of Mansell, it is most
certainly not intended to be. One of the great challenges
facing any F1 driver is to make absolutely sure that he is
in the best car available at any point in history. Mansell
did a fantastic job in this respect and there is no doubt
that his highly motivated and intense approach when it
came to encouraging and cajoling his mechanics and
engineers was highly inspirational.

There are some who certainly recall that working with
Mansell could be a bit of a pain, but none of those who
worked for his success would deny that he brought a lot
to the party and gave ten-tenths effort on almost every
occasion he climbed in behind the wheel.

30. LEWIS HAMILTON (Great Britain)

b. 7.1.1985, Stevenage, England

17 Grands Prix, 4 wins. Career span: 2007 (McLaren).

In a sense it's almost unimaginable that we are talking in
such terms after only one season, but the question still
needs to be confronted. Could Lewis Hamilton develop

into the greatest F1 driver of all time, eclipsing all the previous legends in the sport's history, including even Ayrton Senna, Alain Prost and Michael Schumacher?

That was the tantalising talking point consuming many observers after the 22-year-old British rookie came within a point of winning the world championship at his first attempt, admittedly at the wheel of the superbly competitive McLaren-Mercedes MP4-22.

After the McLaren management took the decision to sign Hamilton to drive alongside Alonso in 2007, they vowed that he would be the best-prepared F1 novice of all time. When he competed in the Australian Grand Prix they wanted to be able to look each other in the eye and know that they couldn't have worked harder to help Lewis at his first race.

Frank Williams summed it up from a rival's perspective. 'I thought after we got rid of Michael [Schumacher], "Now we've got a chance again." But then another super-human turns up,' said Williams. 'Michael was many things, but he was also a very, very simple human. Hamilton is a different character I think, but purely in terms of calibre or quality of skill, what I'm seeing so early in this man's career is remarkable.'

Although some viewed the dominance that Schumacher achieved at times of his career as bad for the sport, Williams thinks that Hamilton is great news for F1 – as he serves to increase its popularity.

'Hamilton is still a baby, so to speak, but dishing out loads of trouble already,' said Williams. 'I mean that in the nicest possible way. I cry he's not in a Williams but I rejoice for F1. I really do.'

So let's ask another question. Could Lewis just develop into the best driver in the business, ignoring his failure to win the championship first time out in 2007? Nobody in their right mind believed his freshman year would be without its setbacks, but the way in which he handled such problems provided us with a further pointer to his future greatness.

Yet from a personal perspective I've been covering F1 for 34 years and I've never seen a debut run which even approached what Hamilton achieved. No question about it, the youngster dropped the ball in both the Chinese and Brazilian Grands Prix, both of which were strategically crucial slips which handed his championship rival Kimi Raikkonen much-needed momentum in the closing stages of their contest. But you just had to pinch yourself and keep on remembering that this was a youngster at the very start of his career in one of the most competitive sports in the world. Hamilton has that special touch, no question.

29. KIMI RAIKKONEN (Finland)

b. 17.10.1979, Espoo, Finland

120 Grands Prix, 15 wins. World champion 2007. Career span: 2001 (Sauber); 2002–06 (McLaren); 2007 (Ferrari).

On the day after the 2007 season finale at the Brazilian Grand Prix, race fans across the world found themselves waking up to a very different world champion to the one that British enthusiasts were waiting to celebrate. Whereas Lewis Hamilton – Britain's top hope for the title – was a media-savvy member of the high technology generation, Raikkonen remains an old-fashioned racing driver out of the heroic mould to whom a beer with his old friends is as important as driving flat-out to Grand Prix glory.

There is very much a touch of James Hunt about Raikkonen. The Finn may not be as obviously extrovert as the 1976 world champion who died of a heart attack in 1993, but Hunt would certainly have approved of reports of Raikkonen's roistering behaviour in a West End club and his reportedly falling asleep outside a Spanish bar clutching an inflatable dolphin.

The third Finn to win the world championship can certainly put his foot down in more ways than one. 'I live my life on my own terms, and that's it,' he said.

Yet for all his obvious zest for life, Raikkonen is a real professional to whom Ferrari paid a reputed $34m a year to prise him away from McLaren. Like Mika Hakkinen before him – who Michael Schumacher confessed was his most formidable rival of all – Raikkonen has that unique blend of raw speed and total control which has been the hallmark of previous generations of Scandinavian racing drivers. Some might say he is abnormally brave, but he also has a self-contained strength of character which makes him almost impervious to the political jockeying which is a regular part of the GP business and which has obviously unseated many more gregarious operators.

Certainly there can be no denying that he is a worthy world champion, winning six of the season's seventeen races, two more than Hamilton and Fernando Alonso and three more than his own team-mate Felipe Massa, who obligingly relinquished the lead at the final round of refuelling stops in the Brazilian race.

Raikkonen confessed that he always believed that he had a chance of winning the world championship, even though at one point in the middle of the season he had fallen to 26 points behind title leader Lewis Hamilton, but he had closed the gap to just seven points by the start of the final race of the year.

At the start of the year he had to sit and watch Massa

win two of the season's first four races as he grappled to get the best out of the Bridgestone tyres, which were new to him after using Michelin rubber on the previous year's McLaren. But victories in the French and British Grands Prix on consecutive weekends reversed that trend and set him back on the road towards the front of the field, which finally paid off to such spectacular effect at Interlagos.

28. KEKE ROSBERG (Finland)

b. 6.12.1948, Stockholm, Sweden

114 Grands Prix, 5 wins. World champion 1982. Career span: 1978 (Theodore); 1979 (Wolf); 1980–81 (Fittipaldi); 1982–85 (Williams); 1986 (McLaren).

This son of a Finnish vet and amateur rally driver had come to front-line international racing quite late in the day. Lars Rosberg would have preferred his son to pursue a career in dentistry or computer programming, but was nevertheless supportive when Keke started kart racing in his teens.

In 1978, Keke won the rain-soaked Silverstone International Trophy race in the Theodore TR1 which was owned by Hong Kong-based entrepreneur Teddy Yip, a hugely passionate motor racing enthusiast. Yet it would take more than another year before he seriously got his foot on the F1 ladder. After the 1979 Monaco Grand Prix, James Hunt decided to quit Walter Wolf's F1 team. And Keke got the job.

Wolf amalgamated with Fittipaldi and eventually closed its doors. But then a lifeline thrown by Frank Williams came in the form of an invitation to a test session at the Paul Ricard circuit in southern France late in 1981.

Williams was also testing the Frenchman Jean-Pierre Jarier as a possible candidate for the job as Carlos Reutemann's team-mate in 1982. But it was Keke who really excited talent scout Charlie Crichton-Stuart and the team's aerodynamicist Frank Dernie.

'It was obvious he was tremendously quick and determined from the outset,' Charlie subsequently recounted. 'On our first night in the hotel down at Ricard he was up until one o'clock drinking with us, and the next morning Frank Dernie suggested: "Let's put this guy on qualifiers and tell him to go for it, without even a lap to warm up." So Keke appeared, bleary-eyed, drinking endless black coffees and smoking about half a dozen Marlboros at once. Into the car and snap! He was instantly quick. A blind, one-eyed monkey could have seen his potential.'

Rosberg won the '82 title on the back of a single victory in the so-called Swiss GP at Dijon-Prenois, but this was a season in which no one driver won more than two races and the Finn's championship battle against the Brabham-mounted Nelson Piquet went right down to the wire at the final race in Las Vegas. Rosberg would stay with Williams through until the end of 1985; theirs was a heady, often stormy partnership and Keke, knowing he was going to race for only one more season after that, decided he would spend that final year at McLaren as Alain Prost's team-mate.

Rosberg would later return to the cockpit racing Group C sports cars for the Peugeot squad and later had a stint at the wheel of a DTM Mercedes touring car. He gave 100 per cent effort to both programmes, just as he had done throughout his F1 career, and the fact of the matter is that Rosberg – like Dan Gurney, just ahead of him in this rating – never managed to deliver the hard results which were promised by his dynamic talent.

27. DAN GURNEY (USA)

b. 13.4.1931, Port Jefferson, New York

86 Grands Prix, 4 wins. Career span: 1959 (Ferrari); 1960 (BRM); 1961–62 (Porsche); 1963–65 (Brabham); 1966–68 (Eagle); 1970 (McLaren).

He may have won only four Grands Prix during his career, but this lanky son of an opera singer is remembered as one of the very finest of his generation. All you basically need to know about Gurney is that the legendary Jim Clark rated him in that exclusive band of genuine competitors. He stands alongside Mario Andretti as the best American F1 driver of all time.

Gurney cut his racing teeth on the Californian sports car scene, after which a spell in Korea with the US military briefly interrupted a steady progression which eventually saw him off to Le Mans in 1958 as a member of Luigi Chinetti's legendary Ferrari squad, the North American Racing Team. That led to an invitation to test for the Prancing Horse at Modena and by 1959 he found himself promoted to the famous F1 team alongside compatriot Phil Hill and Briton Tony Brooks.

The following year he made the disastrous decision to sign for the chaotic BRM squad, but hurriedly rectified the move in '62 when he moved to Porsche and won the French GP at Rouen-les-Essarts in their flat-8-cylinder machine. He would be back at Rouen two years later posting the first GP success for the emergent Brabham squad. He would stay with Jack's team until the end of '65, and while he consistently matched men-of-the-moment Clark and Graham Hill for sheer speed, he never enjoyed the mechanical reliability necessary to string together a championship challenge.

With the change to the 3-litre F1 regulations at the start of 1966, Gurney decided to go it alone with his own world title challenge. He established All American Racers at Santa Ana, California, and laid plans to do both F1 and Indianapolis programmes. It was the first all-US F1 programme since Woolworth stores heir Lance Reventlow launched his abortive Scarab programme the best part of a decade earlier. It would deliver more in the way of hard results than the Scarab, but nowhere near the level of achievement it should have done.

Dan kicked off the Eagle F1 project with an uncompetitive 2.7-litre Climax 4-cylinder engine while the team waited for the all-new Weslake V12 finally to be readied. Thus equipped, Gurney stormed to victory in the 1967 Belgian GP and the Race of Champions. It looked like the start of something big, but the project never quite gelled. Strapped for cash, and with Gurney exhausting himself with too much trans-Atlantic commuting as he tried to hold the two programmes together, the Eagle F1 project finally faded away in mid-1968. Dan was also depressed by Jim Clark's death that spring in a minor league F2 race at Hockenheim.

Despite this, Gurney gave F1 one final throw of the dice in 1970 after the sad demise of Bruce McLaren, being drafted in to fill the void in the team left by the death of their founder. But Dan realised that the spark had gone out. He returned to the USA and never raced again.

26. HERMANN LANG (Germany)

b. 6.4.1909, Bad Cannstatt, Germany; d. 19.10.1987, Bad
Cannstatt

*32 Grands Prix, 6 wins. Career span: 1935–39 (Mercedes);
1953 (Maserati); 1954 (Mercedes).*

Hermann Lang drove his final F1 outing in a Mercedes
W196 in the 1954 German GP, but the brief details
contained above in his career span merely reflect the
twilight moments of a great career eked out in the
opening seasons of the official world championship. Go
back to the immediate pre-war era and Lang was one of
the great Mercedes stars of his generation, winning the
prestigious 1939 European championship, and – but for
the war – many think he would have been the best driver
of a decade in which a more stark conflict took the place
of automotive competition.

By any standards, Lang came up the hard way. In the
early 1930s he had been so short of work that he was
reduced to taking a job as an engine driver on a light rail-
way at a gravel pit near his home. By 1934 he had become
a test driver in the Mercedes-Benz production car department, and was included in a group of drivers invited to
test the Grand Prix cars; two years later he had become
reserve driver for the team. He was coincidentally also
appointed to be foreman of the racing department. He
was emerging as one of the great talents of the Mercedes
team, but Lang's essentially modest nature could be seen
from the fact that his most pressing off-track ambition at
the time was to build a house on a small patch of land
which he had purchased near Stuttgart. 'My mother and
my fiancée shared my pleasure and the sun seemed to

shine on us,' he said charmingly.

Even after dominating the first Grand Prix of the 1937 season at Tripoli, a success which guaranteed his status as a world-class driver, Lang was still quite a shy man and he and his wife Lydia had to be literally coaxed from their hotel room to join in the lavish prize-giving ceremony to toast his splendid success. Later that season a virulent bout of flu kept Lang from competing in the Monaco GP, but he later confessed that he swore at what he regarded as the inadequate radio broadcasts, only to be silenced by his wife saying: 'Now you know how I feel listening to the radio while I am in the pits watching you race.' Lang did not reply, fearing that his wife might throw the radio out of the window if he came up with a clever rejoinder.

Lang clinched the 1939 European championship by winning the Belgian GP at Spa-Francorchamps, the race in which his Mercedes team-mate Dick Seaman was fatally burned in a horrendous accident. One of Lang's final duties before the war started was to travel to London for Seaman's funeral, together with his fellow team drivers from Mercedes and Auto Union.

25. RONNIE PETERSON (Sweden)

b. 14.2.1944, Orebro, Sweden; d. 11.9.1978, Milan

123 Grands Prix, 10 wins. Career span: 1970–72 (March); 1973–76 (Lotus); 1976 (March); 1977 (Tyrrell); 1978 (Lotus).

Ronnie was the son of a provincial Swedish baker, an unlikely background, you might think, for one of the most exciting talents ever to practise the art of opposite-lock motoring in the cockpit of an F1 car. Outwardly he was a tall and mild-mannered fellow who projected a cautiously unruffled charm. But when the visor on the front of his helmet snapped down, Peterson was transformed into a dazzlingly spectacular automotive acrobat.

In a sense, this was the whole point about Peterson. He knew only one way to drive a racing car and that was flat-out. He came into F1 on a three-year contract with the emergent March team at the start of the 1970 season, spending his first year at the wheel of a private March 701 before being promoted to the works team the following year.

In 1971 Ronnie demonstrated his world-class talent with a string of five GP second places, which earned him the status of world championship runner-up behind Jackie Stewart. It was a season in which his star quality was brilliantly underscored by his victory in the European F2 trophy series. Clearly by now he was ready to win Grands Prix, but not until he switched to Lotus in 1973 would he be in the right place at the right time.

Battling his team-mate Emerson Fittipaldi wheel-to-wheel for much of the season, he won the French, Austrian, Italian and US GPs, but the Lotus drivers split their success and it was the retiring Jackie Stewart who dodged through to take the third title crown of his career. By 1974 the Lotus 72 was getting a little long in the tooth, but Peterson still took it to victories in the Monaco, French and Italian races, although Emerson – who had now moved to McLaren – beat him to the title crown.

By the start of the '76 season it was clear that Lotus was in competitive decline, so Ronnie grabbed the opportunity to switch back to March where the user-friendly Type 761 carried him to his third victory in the Italian GP at Monza. Optimistically, he joined the Tyrrell squad for

1977 but their over-complex Maurice Phillippe-designed six-wheeler P34 just wasn't sufficiently competitive, with the result that Ronnie finished a troubled year with many F1 insiders in the pit lane questioning whether he still had the talent to run at the front of the pack.

Determined to prove he was still a potential world championship contender, Ronnie gambled on rejoining Lotus in 1978 – but accepting number two status to Mario Andretti, freely acknowledging that the American driver's great talent at test and development work was responsible for making the new ground-effect Lotus 79 the race-winning tool it was developed into. Ronnie won two races, but died as a result of leg injuries sustained when he crashed going into the first corner at Monza, the scene of those three memorable victories. The F1 community was left bereft at the passing of this fine man.

24. JOHN SURTEES (Great Britain)

b. 11.2.1934, Tatsfield, Surrey, England

111 Grands Prix, 6 wins. World champion 1964. Career span: 1960 (Lotus); 1961 (Cooper); 1963–66 (Ferrari); 1966 (Cooper); 1967–68 (Honda); 1969 (BRM); 1970–72 (Surtees).

John was a deeply committed and very serious-minded competitor. He won seven world championships on two wheels for the legendary MV Agusta motorcycle team before switching to cars in 1960 with brilliant effect. His empathy with all things Italian led to him joining Ferrari in 1963 and he sealed a world championship the following year, becoming the only man so far to win title crowns in both disciplines.

Surtees could be inspirational and frustrating to work for in equal measure. In that sense he was much like Nigel Mansell: imbued with huge self-belief and confident that his way of doing things was the only right way. In 1966 he would leave Ferrari after a falling-out with the Commendatore in circumstances which have never been satisfactorily explained. All that was certain is that this parting of the ways was a loss to both men.

He had been badly injured in a Can-Am sports car accident at Toronto's Mosport Park circuit at the end of 1965 and during the days immediately afterwards it looked as though he might not survive. Yet with the great tenacity and single-mindedness which characterised his career from the start, he pulled himself back from the brink and was ready for the start of 1966, the first season of the new 3-litre F1 regulations.

Ferrari was ready for the off with a new 3-litre V12 at its disposal and all looked promising, but the effectiveness of the Ferrari assault would be undermined – as would become so familiar – with internal dissent and politics. In particular, Surtees fell foul of team manager Eugenio Dragoni who personally championed the cause of his popular team-mate Lorenzo Bandini, a driver with whom Surtees got on well, but who was not really world championship material. Dragoni, however, believed that he was, and worked hard behind the scenes to undermine Surtees' role as team leader, continually trying to advance the theory that the Englishman was not yet fully recovered from his injuries and would probably no longer be a competitive proposition.

Surtees seemingly demolished these reservations by winning the rain-soaked Belgian GP at Spa-Francorchamps in masterly style, but a subsequent row over the driver pairings for the Le Mans 24-hour sports car classic caused Surtees to withdraw from the team on the spot. Mid-season now, he joined the Cooper-Maserati squad, winning the 1966 Mexican GP in their Maserati V12-engined car, after which he embarked on a tiring two seasons trying to make competitive sense of the complex Honda V12 project.

John would score one more GP victory driving for Honda, but that was the sum total of his achievement. Honda pulled out of F1 at the end of 1968 and for 1969 John joined the fading BRM squad. It turned out to be a technical fiasco, so all that was left was for his own Team Surtees organisation to settle down and build its own machines. He built some good F1 and F2 cars in the early 1970s, but never scaled the upper peaks again. In many ways his was a career which was squandered. Sad to relate.

23. GUY MOLL (France)

b. 28.5.1910, Rivet, Algeria; d. 15.8.1934, Pescara, Italy

14 major races, 1 win. Career span: 1932–34 (Bugatti and Alfa Romeo).

Winner of the 1934 Monaco Grand Prix, Guy Moll was hailed by many of his contemporaries, including Enzo Ferrari, as one of the most remarkable talents in the sport's history. More than 50 years later, René Dreyfus, the winner at Monaco in 1930 – the second only such Grand Prix – recalled the young French Algerian in tones so clearly focused it was almost as if he had met his fellow driver the previous day. Yet Moll had been killed in the high summer of '34 on the daunting Pescara road circuit.

'Moll was a freak talent,' Dreyfus reflected to my colleague Nigel Roebuck. 'A Rosemeyer, a Villeneuve, yet his career lasted no time at all, even shorter than poor Gilles. Ferrari always talked about Nuvolari, Moll, Moss and Gilles Villeneuve in the same breath and I would not disagree with that.' Ferrari himself added: 'With the stuff in him to become one of the greatest aces of all time, Moll was, unfortunately, a passing – if memorable – meteor in the motor racing firmament. He met his death at Pescara in 1934 whilst overtaking [Ernst] Henne's Mercedes; he skidded, probably on account of a collision, ran off the road and was killed outright.'

'Together with Moss, he was the only driver worthy of comparison with Nuvolari. In fact, he resembled Nuvolari in certain singular mental traits, in his aggressive spirit, in the calm assurance with which he drove and in the equanimity with which he was prepared to face death.'

From a distance of over 80 years it is difficult in the extreme to get an accurate and touching perspective of this man who all-too-briefly demonstrated his gift for car control on rutted, dusty and poorly surfaced tracks across Europe, at a time when drivers had to struggle dramatically and physically just to keep their slipping and sliding monsters under control. In 1934 the offer came at last for him to join the Scuderia Ferrari to drive their Alfa Romeos – effectively the Milan company's official racing offshoot in the years leading up to the Second World War.

In addition to Moll's victory at Monaco his '34 season was punctuated by an impressive series of top three placings to the point where it was clearly only a matter of time before he added further lustre to his already gilded reputation.

22. NELSON PIQUET (Brazil)

b. 17.8.1952, Rio de Janeiro

204 Grands Prix, 23 wins. World champion 1981, '83 and '87. Career span: 1978 (Ensign and McLaren); 1979–85 (Brabham); 1986–87 (Williams); 1988–89 (Lotus); 1991–92 (Benetton).

This gifted Brazilian was born Nelson Sauto-Maoir, but switched to using his mother's maiden name, Piquet, at an early stage in his career when he wanted to keep the fact that he was motor racing from his parents' attention. If his father had got his way, the young Nelson would have been coached for a life of professional tennis, but the youngster found the lure of high octane competition just too much to resist.

By any objective standards, Piquet was a great F1 driver, although he was very much the cool poker player in the sense that he would work assiduously during testing to build up a technical performance edge which he usually tended to keep to himself, rather than share it with his various team-mates over the years.

After making his way up from a grounding in kart racing, Nelson was dominating the British F3 championship scene by the end of 1978 and made some intermittent F1 outings with a couple of minor teams by the end of that year. Bernie Ecclestone quickly homed in on Nelson's innate talent, signing him to drive for the Brabham team from the start of 1979. He stayed there until the start of 1986 when – having won two world championships – he switched to the Williams-Honda squad alongside Nigel Mansell. Despite a tense and bitter rivalry with the feisty British driver, Nelson bagged another title before switching to Lotus, and later Benetton, where he finished his distinguished F1 career.

Many F1 insiders felt that Piquet was never more comfortable than during his time with the Brabham team. Ecclestone never overpaid him, but always indulged him just enough to ensure that his competitive motivation kept simmering on the hob. His relationship with Gordon Murray, the legendary Brabham chief designer, was closely collaborative and the mechanics held him in very high regard. In short, this was very much a mutual admiration society cast within the operational parameters of a lean and taut racing infrastructure.

To a large extent, Piquet was Brabham throughout the early 1980s and it worked with a seamless efficiency. Yet when Nelson dropped the bombshell that he was leaving the team at the end of 1985 to partner Nigel Mansell at Williams, the pit lane was stunned.

The Piquet/Mansell rivalry, intense though it was, always manage to contain itself one step short of physical confrontation. 'It once got out of hand in the cabin [team office] at Mexico City after the 1987 race when they slagged each other off face to face,' said Frank Williams.

'They never came near to punch-ups, it was all "if you think that was close, wait until next time", but they were still pumped up after the race, the adrenalin was still flowing. They were professionals and realised they both had to cross the finishing line in order to score points.'

21. JOCHEN RINDT (Austria)

b. 18.4.1942, Mainz-am-Rhein, Germany; d. 5.9.1970, Monza

60 Grands Prix, 6 wins. World champion 1970. Career span:
1964 (Rob Walker); 1965–67 (Cooper); 1968 (Brabham);
1969–70 (Lotus).

Rindt's parents were killed in a bombing raid on Hamburg when he was only a few weeks old, so he was brought up by his maternal grandparents in the Austrian city of Graz. He grew up with a wild and rebellious streak which ensured that he was an intensely independent operator for much of his career, brimming with self-confidence and natural talent.

Jochen exploded to the forefront of public attention by winning the 1964 London Trophy on the tight little Crystal Palace circuit, a summer afternoon on which he beat all the established stars and put his name in the frame as a likely tip for future success.

He made his F1 debut driving Rob Walker's Brabham-BRM in the first non-championship Austrian GP on the bumpy Zeltweg aerodrome circuit, after which he signed a three-year deal which saw him driving for the now-fading Cooper F1 team through to the end of 1967. At this point he switched to Brabham, an apparently ideal move to judge by the fact that their Repco-engined cars had powered to the last two title crowns. Sadly, the season was marred by seemingly endless engine troubles and Rindt had to be content with one third place in the opening race of the season in South Africa.

Jochen admired Jack Brabham, trusting his team's dependable engineering standards. He felt safe and secure at the wheel of their cars. But after Jimmy Clark's death in April 1968 it seemed only a matter of time before Lotus boss Colin Chapman made a pitch for Rindt's services.

Yet not until he drove for Lotus in 1969 did Jochen finally score his first GP victory, after years of trying. He

ALAN HENRY

died at Monza practising for the following year's Italian GP when a brake shaft broke on his Lotus 72, leaving his wife Nina – a former international model – and a three-year-old daughter, Natascha. By then he had amassed sufficient points to ensure that he would claim the dubious distinction of becoming the sport's first – and so far thankfully only – posthumous world champion.

Jochen was also a close friend of Bernie Ecclestone, who negotiated his contracts with both the Brabham and Lotus teams. During his time at Lotus, Jochen and Bernie used to drive Colin Chapman round the bend by their habit of playing gin rummy right up to – and sometimes beyond – the moment when the Lotus boss required his star driver to climb in the cockpit and strut his stuff. Most people who knew him felt that Jochen was a far-sighted businessman who could visualise a life well beyond F1. Probably in partnership with Bernie.

20. NIKI LAUDA (Austria)

b. 22.2.1949, Vienna

171 Grands Prix, 25 wins. World champion 1975, '77 and '84. Career span: 1971–72 (March); 1973 (BRM); 1974–77 (Ferrari); 1978–79 (Brabham); 1982–85 (McLaren).

Outwardly ascetic and rather formal, the true personality of Niki Lauda couldn't be further from this stereotyped image. Niki served his motor racing apprenticeship in the early 1970s when the offbeat humour of John Cleese and *Monty Python's Flying Circus* was very much in vogue. You might find it difficult to imagine a future triple world champion joining in with the March mechanics shouting 'albatross' or 'gannet on a stick' but you can take it from me that's how it was.

When Niki made his F2 debut in 1971, paying March Engineering £8,500 for the privilege of contesting the prestigious European Trophy series – then the equivalent of GP2, the present feeder series for Grand Prix racing – he was a rather frail and slight-looking individual. There was precious little evidence to suggest that he would develop into one of the sport's most calm and focused technocrats, a driver who melded natural skill and mechanical sensitivity into an unbeatable competitive cocktail.

He was also commercially bold to the point of reckless-ness. In order to finance his 1972 season he borrowed an astronomic £35,000 from an Austrian bank to fund a place in the March F1 team. Truth be told, this was money down the drain, but thanks to some negotiating ingenuity he worked his way into a BRM drive for the following year. He briefly ran third at Monaco until the gearbox broke, but that was enough to catch the attention of Enzo Ferrari. For 1974 he slipped behind the wheel of one of the scarlet cars from Maranello and was on his way to the first of his two Ferrari championships, achieved in 1975 and '77.

He left Ferrari to join Bernie Ecclestone's Brabham team and then retired from driving from mid-1979 through to the start of 1982, when McLaren boss Ron Dennis tempted him back into the cockpit, a move which laid the foundations for his fourth championship title in 1984. He finally retired for good at the end of '85, since when he has occupied himself in the aviation industry, first with Lauda Air and latterly with his budget airline Niki, for which he pilots an Airbus A139 as one of the regular captains.

On a personal level, Niki shrugged aside his burns

sustained at Nürburgring in 1976 with total stoicism. But he was deeply shaken by the crash of one of his Lauda Air Boeing 767s over Thailand in 1992 with the loss of over 200 lives. 'If I want to risk my life in a racing car, that's one thing,' he said. 'But if passengers buy a ticket on my airline and don't come back it's totally unacceptable.' The aircraft had suffered a failure, and he pursued Boeing on the matter of a legal settlement for all the victims with the single-minded tenacity that he'd applied to his race driving.

19. MARIO ANDRETTI (USA)

b. 28.2.1940, Montona, Italy

128 Grands Prix, 12 wins. World champion 1978. Career span: 1968–69 (Lotus); 1970 (March); 1971–72 (Ferrari); 1974–76 (Parnelli); 1976–80 (Lotus); 1981 (Alfa Romeo); 1982 (Williams and Ferrari).

Mario Andretti's life story has about it the essence of the great American dream. He was born near Trieste in the early months of the Second World War and his family spent the first seven years of his life in a displaced persons' camp, eventually emigrating to the USA in 1955.

Mario, brought up on a diet of Alberto Ascari and the legendary Mille Miglia road race, later admitted that the prospect of leaving Italy horrified him. He thought he might never see motor racing again, but, as history happily relates, he and his brother Aldo picked up the threads of their passion for the sport once they arrived on the opposite side of the Atlantic.

After cutting his teeth on the unyieldingly intense dirt

track ovals which formed the bedrock of US motor racing, Mario would contest the Indy 500 for the first time in 1965. Three years later it seemed as though he was poised to challenge for F1 glory when he started his works Lotus 49B from pole position for the US GP at Watkins Glen, an achievement which led to his being nominated as the team's third driver for the following season, although he would have to wait another two years before winning his first F1 championship round.

Mario won the Indy 500 for his first and only time in 1969, triumphed in the '71 South African GP for Ferrari and went on to win the world championship for Lotus in 1978. In 1981 he made a catastrophic switch to Alfa Romeo, scoring his only points of the season with a fourth-place finish at Long Beach, the opening race of the year.

He quit full-time F1 at the end of that season, but guested for Williams at Long Beach the following year and was lured back to make an emotional appearance in the Italian GP at Monza where he qualified his 126C2 on pole and finished third. Retirement with a suspension breakage finally wound down the curtain on his illustrious F1 career.

One of the most versatile drivers ever to sit in a racing car, as well as one of the most civil and courteous, he was neverthless no soft touch.

He had no compunction about overtaking his son Michael's misfiring machine on the run-up to the che-quered flag in the 1986 Portland CART race, prompting the younger Andretti to air the view that it might have been nice if his Old Man had allowed him to squeeze home the winner.

Mario's eyes narrowed. 'That's not the way it works, Michael,' he said drily.

18. JACK BRABHAM (Australia)

b. 12.4.1926, Hurstville, nr Sydney

126 Grands Prix, 14 wins. World champion 1959, '60 and '66. Career span: 1955–61 (Cooper); 1962–70 (Brabham).

One of motor racing's great practical down-to-earth heroes, Jack Brabham's career efforts were not only rewarded with three world championship crowns but he gained the third at the wheel of a car bearing his own name. This in itself was a unique achievement, made all the more satisfying by the fact that Jack was 40 when he took his last title – and regarded as over-the-hill by many motor racing commentators.

In fact Jack drove on competitively until the age of 44, finally ringing down the shutters on a remarkable career at the end of the 1970 season. All in all, it was quite a story for this grandson of a cockney who emigrated to Australia back in 1885. Jack was born in an outer Sydney suburb, the son of a greengrocer, and it was while working as a youngster on his father's trucks and cars in a local garage that he became imbued with the mechanical resourcefulness which was to become the defining hallmark of his career.

Brabham cut his teeth in the hotly contested domestic Australian championship scene, well ahead of his time when he attracted Redex sponsorship for his Cooper-Bristol as early as 1954. The motor sporting authorities in Australia became very sniffy indeed about this, and Brabham was made to remove the identification from the flanks of his car. That attitude didn't bother Jack for long. By the end of '54 he was already making plans to head for England, where he arrived in time to make his F1 debut in the following year's British GP at Aintree driving a central-seat Cooper sports car.

Thereafter he rode the crest of the wave as Cooper boldly rewrote the parameters of F1 car performance with their agile central-engined machines. Granted, it may have been Stirling Moss who posted the marque's maiden victory in Rob Walker's car at Buenos Aires in 1958, but once Jack got into his stride through '59 there was simply no stopping him.

With both Vanwall and Maserati out of the picture, Ferrari still wrestling with their outdated Dino 246 and Lotus still to come to flower, Cooper relished a two-year window of opportunity during which Brabham won seven races and his first two championships. It was a classic case of the right man being in the right car at the right moment. By the end of 1961 Jack had decided that the time was ripe to set up on his own, and the first Brabham F1 car duly raced the following year's GP.

Not until the '64 French GP at Rouen did a Brabham F1 car win its first championship round, in this case thanks to the efforts of American Dan Gurney, but Jack was fully prepared for the new 3-litre F1 regulations which came in at the start of 1966. With the collaboration of Repco, the Australian replacement car component company, he developed a 3-litre F1 engine based around a lightweight Oldsmobile cylinder block. The rest, as they say, is history.

17. EMERSON FITTIPALDI (Brazil)

b. 12.12.1946, São Paolo, Brazil

144 Grands Prix, 14 wins. World champion 1972 and '74.

Career span: 1970–73 (Lotus); 1974–75 (McLaren);
1976–80 (Fittipaldi).

Emerson's father Wilson Fittipaldi senior was one of
Brazil's foremost motor sporting journalists and broad-
casters, stretching back to Fangio's emergent years racing
in Europe in the early 1950s. That gave Emerson
Fittipaldi the best possible launch pad for his own motor
racing aspirations.

Wilson Snr and his wife Juzy encouraged the racing
interests of both their sons, Emerson contesting no fewer
than 144 Grand Prix starts and winning 14 races on his
way to two world championships in 1972 (Lotus) and
1974 (McLaren). Later he was twice winner of the Indy
500. To this day, Emerson continues to exude huge
charisma and star quality.

After Piers Courage was killed in the 1970 Dutch GP at
Zandvoort, Frank Williams tried hard to sign Emerson
to drive his de Tomaso for the balance of the season,
but there was no way this was going to happen. Colin
Chapman had him firmly locked into a 'Lotus only'
contract and quickly affirmed his confidence in the
young Brazilian by entering him in a Lotus 49C at the
British GP at Brands Hatch. Two months later, team
leader Jochen Rindt was killed at Monza and Emerson
found himself catapulted into that vacant role, winning
the US GP at Watkins Glen, only his fourth-ever GP.

Despite losing some career momentum in 1971 due
to a road accident, Emerson bounced back to win the
'72 world championship, only for Chapman to recruit
the dynamic Ronnie Peterson to the team line-up the
following year. Emerson welcomed Ronnie as an old
friend, but with some obvious reservations about his
blinding speed and car control. As things transpired,
there wasn't enough room for both of them in the team

and Emerson left for McLaren at the end of the season, duly winning his second world championship in 1974.

Only when he took the largely emotional decision to switch to his brother Wilson's Fittipaldi Automotive team did Emerson's career lose its momentum and, apart from a brilliant second place to Reutemann's Ferrari at Rio in 1978, the best days of his world championship campaigning receded quickly in his personal rear view mirror.

Emerson's grandson Pietro, son of his daughter Juliane, is now ten and racing karts, while another daughter, Tatiana, is married to the one-time Arrows F1 driver Max Papis, and their son Mario Fittipaldi Papis was born in July 2006. Emerson's elder brother Wilson – three years his senior – contested 36 Grands Prix in the 1970s, his best placing being a fifth at Nürburgring just ahead of his brother in the 1973 German GP driving a Brabham BT42. Wilson junior's son Christian contested 40 Grands Prix driving for both Minardi and Arrows, with three fourth places to his credit, before moving to the USA where he has raced Champcars and NASCAR. Quite some dynasty for the delightful Emerson to rule over!

16. ACHILLE VARZI (Italy)

b. 8.8.1904, Galliate, nr Milan; d. 30.6.1948, Berne, Switzerland

25 major race wins. Career span: 1928–29 (Alfa Romeo); 1930 (Alfa Romeo/Maserati); 1931–33 (Bugatti); 1934 (Alfa Romeo); 1935–36 (Auto Union); 1937 (Maserati); 1947–48 (Alfa Romeo).

Varzi was one of the sport's greatest talents who was eventually laid low by drug addiction and its attendant myriad problems. A motorcycle racing contemporary of Tazio Nuvolari, he switched to car racing in 1926 at the wheel of a Type 37 Bugatti and immediately joined up with his fellow Italian, although it was soon clear that there wouldn't be enough room for these two highly motivated men in this single organisation, and by the middle of the 1928 season Varzi decided to go it alone, acquiring an Alfa Romeo P2 from the great Giuseppe Campari.

Unfortunately Varzi's reputation was stained in 1933 when he became complicit in a controversial row at the Tripoli GP in North Africa which was being run in conjunction with a state lottery, some 30 tickets being drawn to correspond with the 30 starters. It appeared that an Italian lumber merchant called Enrico Rivio had purchased the ticket bearing Varzi's name, which stood to win him about 8 million lire – around £1m by today's standards – if his driver duly delivered the requisite result.

In the event, Nuvolari ran out of fuel coming up to the finishing line on the final lap, handing Varzi a fortunate, if highly dubious, victory. Thus did Signor Rivio claim his prize purse, which he duly shared with Varzi and the other competitors involved in the obvious deception. But this controversy was quickly swept behind Varzi who, by now at the very peak of his racing reputation, joined the Auto Union team in 1935 where he was confidently expected to thrive, even taking into consideration the arrival of the spectacular young German rising star Bernd Rosemeyer in the line-up.

Yet there were to be other problems attendant on Varzi joining Auto Union. The 30-year-old Italian would fall in love with Ilse Pietsch, the young wife of his 22-year-old team-mate Paul Pietsch. At the end of that first season,

Pietsch left Auto Union and his former wife moved in with Varzi. During their time together it seems that Ilse introduced him to the questionable attractions of morphia, and in a short time it seemed as though Varzi underwent a complete personality change, this reserved man who kept himself very much to himself now apparently given to meaningless and garrulous chatter. His brilliant racing career eventually fell apart in the run-up to the Second World War, but in 1946, at the age of 42, Varzi set about restoring his reputation. He duly joined the works Alfa Romeo team, but practising for the 1948 Swiss GP at Berne's Bremgarten circuit he spun and hit a kerb. His Alfa 158 flipped over at scarcely more than walking pace and Varzi was killed instantly.

15. CARLOS REUTEMANN (Argentina)

b. 12.4.1942, Santa Fe, Argentina

146 Grands Prix, 12 wins. Career span: 1972–76 (Brabham); 1976–78 (Ferrari); 1979 (Lotus); 1980–82 (Williams).

This serious-minded Argentinian driver remained something of a distant enigma throughout a long and distinguished F1 career during which he combined moments of dazzling genius with disappointingly lacklustre showings. On a personal level away from the cockpit, his gentle and charming personality was often concealed behind a mask of deep thought and intense concentration.

Yet make no mistake about it, on his day, Reutemann was simply inspirational. He originally turned up on the European scene in 1970 as a member of the National

F2 team and nearly pipped Ronnie Peterson for the following year's European Championship. In 1972 he qualified his Brabham BT34 on pole position for his first GP outing in front of his home crowd at Buenos Aires and seemed set for a high flying future. Disappointingly, he never won in Argentina. He should have done in '74, but the Brabham team had apparently made a mistake fuelling his car and left one churn out prior to the start. Carlos' Brabham BT44 ran out of juice with just over a lap to go while running away from the pack.

He switched from Brabham to Ferrari from late 1976 to 1978, pairing up with Niki Lauda in the Maranello line-up in '77, which was an uneasy alliance. The two men did not really hit it off together, perhaps because of their diametrically opposed personalities. Reutemann won only the Brazilian GP that year, but won four races on Michelin rubber in 1978. He then made a mistake in moving to Lotus, and finally – more sensibly – to Williams in 1980. In 1981 he stood poised on the verge of the title crown, only to inexplicably relinquish his chance to Nelson Piquet in the final race at Las Vegas.

Two races into the 1982 season, Carlos Reutemann retired from the cockpit for good. He never went back on that spontaneous decision, although he would subsequently acknowledge that he had given up too soon. Quite why he did it is a secret which may never be revealed, but there is no doubt that his departure from the starting grids robbed F1 of one of its most outstanding contemporary talents.

After retiring from the sport, Carlos went into politics and became one of the leading politicians in Argentina as governor of the Sante Fe province and later as a senator.

14. TONY BROOKS (Great Britain)

b. 25.2.1932, Dukinfield, Cheshire, England

38 Grands Prix, 6 wins. Career span: 1956 (BRM); 1957–58 (Vanwall); 1959 (Ferrari); 1960 (Yeoman Credit); 1961 (BRM).

Tony Brooks was a great F1 driver, even though his self-effacing and naturally modest nature would leave him slightly embarrassed in the face of such a stark pronouncement. In retirement he is so reserved that it is sometimes difficult to appreciate that this is the man who mastered Spa, the Nürburgring and Monza at the wheel of a Vanwall in the golden summer of 1958.

The son of a dentist, Brooks also qualified in dentistry. In fact, on the flight down to Sicily for the 1955 Syracuse GP, the race he won for Connaught which suddenly and dramatically raised his own personal profile, he was glued to his text books as he studied for his finals. He did so on the return trip as well, although the intervening few days had seen him enter the history books as the man who gave Britain its first continental victory since Sir Henry Seagrave won the San Sebastian GP in a Sunbeam 31 years before.

In 1956 Brooks accepted an invitation to join BRM, but when it came to it he contested only the British GP, in which he came close to disaster. The car's throttle stuck open at Abbey Curve and the car turned over, throwing out its driver before bursting into flames in the middle of the circuit. For Tony the legacy was a badly broken jaw, but he was happy to settle for that in the knowledge that things could have been much worse.

Brooks joined Vanwall in 1957 but his season was

compromised by an accident at Le Mans where he rolled his Aston Martin, though he shared with Moss the winning car in the British GP at Aintree. It was in 1958 that Brooks came into his own, his meticulous style and sure touch earning him superb victories in the Belgian, German and Italian GPs, all classic races on three of the most exacting circuits in the world.

After Vanwall withdrew at the end of 1958 he joined Ferrari, but his rigid self-discipline and religious conviction ironically conspired to undermine his chances of winning the world championship. On the opening lap of the US GP at Sebring he was bumped from behind by his team-mate Wolfgang von Trips and the Englishman pulled in to check for damage.

This may have cost Brooks a shot at the title, but to do anything else would have been out of step with his personal philosophy. In the end he finished third, with Brabham pushing his out-of-fuel Cooper home fourth to take the first of his three championships.

By the end of '59, Brooks's thoughts were turning towards retirement and the further development of his garage business at Byfleet, close to the old Brooklands banking. Driving an uncompetitive Cooper-Climax for Yeoman Credit in 1960 and a gutless four-cylinder BRM in 1961 rounded off a distinguished career for this fine man, albeit on a rather anti-climactic note.

13. CHRIS AMON (New Zealand)

b. 20.7.1943, Bulls, North Island, NZ

96 Grands Prix. Career span: 1963 (Lola and Lotus); 1964–65 (Lotus); 1966 (Cooper); 1967–69 (Ferrari); 1970

*(March); 1971–72 (Matra); 1973 (Tecno); 1974 (Amon and
BRM); 1975–76 (Ensign).*

He never won a single Grand Prix, never mind a world
championship, but no serious student of F1 history
would dispute the fact that Amon was a world-class driver
fully capable of competing with the best of them. Yet
when it came to taking strategic career decisions, this
mild-mannered son of a prosperous New Zealand sheep
farmer could, time and again, be relied on to pluck the
joker from the bottom of the pack.

His career in the F1 front line thus went sadly
unfulfilled. Yet at his absolute peak he was hailed by
legendary Ferrari engineer Mauro Forghieri as being in
much the same class as Jimmy Clark when it came to
sheer delicacy of touch and pure artistry behind the
wheel. His relations with Ferrari had his trademark
disaster stamped all over them. By the summer of 1969,
driven to the edge of frustration by the unreliability of
their V12 engines, Chris decided instead to sign for the
fledgling March team the following year. It was absolutely
typical that the moment he turned his back on them, the
famous Italian team kicked off possibly its most successful
era with the flat-12-engined 312s.

After making his name competing in national races in
New Zealand – his father Ngaio was wealthy enough to
buy him an old Cooper-Climax single seater back in 1960
– he was eventually spotted by British F1 private entrant
Reg Parnell, who offered a deal which saw him plucked
from this domestic backwater and installed in the cockpit
of an F1 Lola-Climax at the age of nineteen.

By '67 he was a member of the works Ferrari team, but
it always seemed that Grand Prix glory would remain
tantalisingly out of reach. In the '68 British GP at Brands
Hatch he briefly slipped ahead of Jo Siffert's winning

Rob Walker team Lotus 49B, but remained a couple of seconds adrift at the chequered flag. Two years later at Spa, the BRM P153 of Pedro Rodriguez displayed a similar burst of mechanical reliability to head home Amon's March by a similar margin. He would later dominate the 1972 French GP for Matra, storming away from the field at Clermont-Ferrand. Only for a punctured tyre to intervene ...

When Matra withdrew from F1 at the end of 1972, Chris took another catastrophic career wrong turning by signing for the hopeless Italian Tecno team. You simply couldn't imagine that things could get worse, but they did. Amon embarked on a hopelessly underfinanced programme to build his own F1 machine, which was as absurdly unreliable as it was punishingly costly.

Chris's final attempt to qualify for a Grand Prix came at the Mosport Park circuit near Toronto in 1976 when his uncompetitive Wolf-Williams spun and was T-boned by another car. The following year he returned to the family farm with his wife Tish, where they live happily to this day.

12. GILLES VILLENEUVE (Canada)

b. 18.1.1950, Berthierville, Quebec; d. 8.5.1982, Zolder, Belgium

67 Grands Prix, 6 wins. Career span: 1977 (McLaren); 1978–82 (Ferrari).

This tiny French-Canadian was one of those rare personalities who became an unquestioned legend in his own lifetime. Gilles was cast from an heroic mould, his fearless and undaunted approach to his chosen profession giving rise to more discussion and debate than any of his contemporaries. There were some who thought he was wonderful, embodying all those romantically traditional qualities on which the sport's history is constructed. Others rejected his tyre-smoking opposite lock antics as a huge waste of time.

Villeneuve rocketed to international prominence when he won the Formula Atlantic race at the Trois Rivières street circuit on the banks of the St Lawrence river in 1976. World champion-elect James Hunt was also contesting this race, and the big-hearted Englishman went straight back to the McLaren F1 team with the recommendation that they keep a close eye on this bright young rising star. In Hunt's mind there was not a shred of doubt that Villeneuve was F1 material in the making.

Gilles' big chance in the F1 front line came in the '77 British GP at Silverstone. Invited to drive a third works McLaren entry, one of the older M23 chassis, he acquitted himself respectably by qualifying in ninth place and then racing competitively to finish tenth despite an unscheduled pit stop. Strangely, McLaren's management passed up the chance of signing the young Canadian at the end of the season, preferring the admittedly very pleasant Patrick Tambay. Instead, Gilles replaced the retiring Niki Lauda at Ferrari and immediately made himself at home in F1 at the start of the following year.

It took Villeneuve only to the third race of 1978 to lead commandingly. But his hopes of guiding the Ferrari 312T3 to victory through the streets of Long Beach were thwarted when he crashed after tripping over tail-ender Clay Regazzoni's Shadow. But by the end of the season he'd successfully broken his duck with a splendid win in the inaugural Canadian GP held at Montreal's Île Nôtre-Dame circuit, again at the wheel of the 312T3.

In 1979 he was paired with Jody Scheckter in the Maranello line-up and, armed with the new Ferrari 312T4, added further wins to his CV at Kyalami, Long Beach and Watkins Glen. From the start of that year Gilles fully appreciated that he was to be cast in a supporting role to his South African colleague, who had been signed up as number one. Keeping that in mind, he displayed his integrity by following scrupulously in Jody's wheel tracks to finish second in the Italian GP at Monza, knowing that all he had to do was to ignore team orders and overtake the South African in order to claim the world championship for himself.

Yet there seemed no immediate prospect of building on this promise for 1980 with the uncompetitive Ferrari 312T5. The year after that, the newly conceived turbo Ferrari 126CK also proved a less-than-competitive offering, but Gilles rose to the occasion in fine fashion to post heroic wins at Monaco and Jarama. On most occasions he easily eclipsed his new team-mate Didier Pironi, yet the Frenchman would turn out to be the architect of catastrophe the following year when he ignored team orders to win the San Marino GP at Imola. Two weeks later Gilles crashed to his death at Zolder, trying to match Pironi's lap times as they battled for grid positions at the Belgian Grand Prix.

11. MICHAEL SCHUMACHER (Germany)

b. 31.1.1969, Hurth-Hermulheim, Germany

249 Grands Prix, 91 wins. World champion 1994, '95, 2000,

'01, '02, '03 and '04. Career span: 1991 (Jordan and Benetton); 1992–95 (Benetton); 1996–2006 (Ferrari).

Michael Schumacher's confidence was for years firmly buttressed by the unwavering support and confidence he enjoyed from a small group of hard-line Ferrari loyalists who believed that his unique talent enabled him to ride out the short-term disruptions generated by the ebb and flow of racing fortunes.

Michael's was an extraordinary talent and the statistical record he wrote into the F1 history books is unlikely ever to be bettered. Yet despite being a devoted family man away from the circuit, once strapped into the cockpit of his car he was a ruthless and uncompromisingly competitive operator who took few hostages and was seldom far from the epicentre of any controversy which might be enveloping the sport at any particular time.

Schumacher's strengths were built around an uncompromising and perfectionist streak. His talent first emerged when he was driving for the Sauber-Mercedes sports car team in the early 1990s. Ross Brawn, then technical director of the rival Silk Cut-Jaguar team, was intrigued by this young German who consistently showed himself to be quicker than his more experienced team-mates while at the same time using significantly less fuel. Brawn, of course, would not have to wait long before learning about Michael first-hand as they collaborated to brilliant effect at both Benetton and Ferrari.

Schumacher always deployed that brilliance to ruthless effect. To him, winning was everything, the underlying raison d'être for his presence in the cockpit of an F1 car. And if harnessing every advantage available to him meant ensuring his Ferrari team-mates Eddie Irvine, Rubens Barrichello and Felipe Massa played the deferential role of a supplicant, then that's how it would be. Why, he wondered, would anybody do it differently? Or indeed frown at it?

There are those who believe that he stayed around perhaps a couple of years too long. If Schumacher's reputation was blotted by his memorable collision with Damon Hill at Adelaide in 1994, or his tangle with Jacques Villeneuve at Jerez three years later, the general consensus was that he had gone too far – even by his own standards – when he deliberately skidded to a halt in the middle of the track during qualifying at Monaco in 2006, thereby thwarting his rival Fernando Alonso's bid for pole position.

Yet Schumacher certainly deserves his place in the pantheon of motor sporting greats for the manner in which he helped revive the Ferrari team fortunes in the late 1990s, laying the foundations for the longest period of sustained success ever achieved by the Prancing Horse.

10. MIKA HAKKINEN (Finland)

b. 28.9.1968, Helsinki

161 Grands Prix, 20 wins. World champion 1998 and '99. Career span: 1991–92 (Lotus); 1993–2001 (McLaren).

You just knew that Mika was made of the right stuff when he outqualified his McLaren team leader Ayrton Senna for the 1993 Portuguese GP at Estoril. Concealing his irritation, Ayrton had to admit that he was impressed. Seven years later, the Finn pulled the overtaking move of the decade at Spa-Francorchamps as he and Michael Schumacher went either side of Ricardo Zonta's

BAR-Honda as they lapped the slower car. Concealing his irritation, Michael had to admit that he was impressed.

It was rare moments of unfettered genius like this that make me place Hakkinen slightly ahead of Schumacher in this rating. There was always something raw and unfettered about Mika's talent – a touch of the Gilles Villeneuve about him, if you like – and always the feeling that there was something utterly spontaneous about that magic.

In some ways he was very like Schumacher indeed; Mika's loyalty to McLaren was very much an uncon-ditional two-way street, much like Michael's commitment to Ferrari. In Mika's case it was strengthened beyond challenge after he crashed heavily due to a puncture during practice for the 1995 Australian GP at Adelaide. For a couple of days his life seemed to hang in the balance, and his recovery to competitive form was both harder and more protracted than we all realised at the time. Unquestionably it forged a close personal relationship with the McLaren boss Ron Dennis which other drivers, most notably David Coulthard, found it impossible to emulate. Coulthard was later requested by team orders to hand Hakkinen victory in both the 1997 European and 1998 Australian GPs, episodes which understandably irk the Scottish driver to this day, although the McLaren management have no doubts that they made a fair decision on both occasions.

Two world championship titles attested to Hakkinen's driving genius. He was one of those rare talents who always seemed to deliver ten-tenths while still leaving a small margin in reserve. He was also one of that elite handful who were prepared to go wheel-to-wheel with Michael Schumacher and sit it out with the German Ferrari ace, and had it not been for a crucial engine failure in the 2000 US GP, Mika might well have scored a hat-trick of championships.

After retiring from F1 he was understandably restless without his racing and in 2005 decided to return to contest the DTM touring car series for Mercedes-Benz, racing for three seasons in this close-fought category before finally calling it a day at the end of 2007.

When Schumacher announced his retirement at the end of 2006 he freely admitted that 'some of his battles with Mika' were among his most pleasurable memories of his time in the F1 business. Compliments rarely come much bigger than that.

9. TAZIO NUVOLARI (Italy)

b. 18.11.1892, Mantua, Italy; d. 11.8.1953, Mantua

75 Grands Prix, 11 wins. Career span: 1934 (Maserati); 1935–37 (Alfa Romeo); 1938–39 (Auto Union).

Nuvolari stamped his mastery on the motor racing history books by winning the 1935 German GP at the Nürburgring at the wheel of an Alfa Romeo P3 fielded by the Scuderia Ferrari. In doing so, the little Italian humbled both the Auto Union and Mercedes teams – particularly the former, as his rivals Achille Varzi and Hans Stuck had privately conspired to keep Nuvolari out of the team at the beginning of that season.

Circumstance therefore effectively dictated that Nuvolari signed up with Ferrari's official Alfa team, and by the time he squared up to the Silver Arrows at the Nürburgring he had already won four races for the Italian team. However, these were regarded as relatively minor events as the German teams had not entered. Under the circumstances it was easy to see why they felt pretty confident on the eve of the most prestigious race on their calendar.

In the opening stages of the race Nuvolari was down in sixth place as Rudi Caracciola led comfortably in his Mercedes ahead of the Auto Union driven by Bernd Rosemeyer. Gradually Tazio worked his way through to third place but his prospects seemed to have evaporated completely when a pressure refuelling pump failed and he lost more than a minute in the pits while his mechanics refuelled his car from churns. The unscheduled delay dropped him from first to sixth place, and while he clawed his way back to second by the start of the final lap, it seemed there was no way in which he could undermine the winning advantage built up by Mercedes star Manfred von Brauchitsch.

Yet von Brauchitsch had been over-driving his car quite dramatically, much to the detriment of its tyres, one of which flew apart mid-way round the final lap, presenting Nuvolari with a superb victory on a plate. This was slightly embarrassing for the organisers, who hadn't bothered to dig out a recording of the Italian national anthem. Not that they needed to worry; Nuvolari always brought his own copy of the Marcia Reale to the circuits for good luck.

Twelve years later and Nuvolari was ageing fast, dogged by the effects of the TB-related illness which would carry him to his grave in 1953. Against the advice of his doctors he took the decision to drive in the 1948 Mille Miglia at the wheel of one of Piero Dusio's Cisitalias, but the car was not ready in time. Enzo Ferrari stepped in and provided him with a car at the last moment.

What followed was almost impossible to believe. By the time the field reached Ravenna, Nuvolari was in the lead.

At Rome he was even further ahead, although his car had lost one mudguard and its bonnet. Nevertheless, by the time he reached Florence on the return leg he was half an hour in the lead. Then at Reggio Emilia he spun to a halt with a broken spring; drained and exhausted, the driver was led away to rest in a nearby hospital.

Enzo Ferrari visited him in a bid to boost his spirits, telling him that there was always next year's race to look forward to. 'Ferrari,' replied Nuvolari, 'at our age there aren't many days like this left. Remember that, and try to enjoy them as much as you can.'

8. JACKIE STEWART (Great Britain)

b. 11.6.1939, Dumbarton, Scotland

99 Grands Prix, 27 wins. World champion 1969, '71 and '73. Career span: 1965–67 (BRM); 1968–69 (Tyrrell Matra); 1970 (Tyrrell March and Tyrrell); 1971–73 (Tyrrell).

Thirty-four years have now passed since Jackie retired at the end of a career which yielded three world championships, but he is now more prominent a figure on the international motor racing scene than he ever was in his motor racing heyday. As one of the sport's most informed observers and influential advisors, he has worked for a wide range of global corporations as an international sporting ambassador.

Yet such were Stewart's achievements in other areas of motorsport that it is all too easy to overlook his impressive racing career. Far more significant is the fact that he debunked the myth that racing drivers should be devil-may-care extroverts to whom death or injury was something they should embrace without question as an automatic part of their calling. He was the driving force behind sweeping safety improvements, an attitude which did not always find favour with the purists by whom he was much maligned as a result. He always made a very good friend and a very bad enemy.

Stewart originally displayed his sporting prowess in the world of shooting. His elder brother Jimmy raced sports cars with distinction, but as far as their parents were concerned this was already one racing driver too many in the family. Jackie was written off as a dunce in his youth – only years later being diagnosed as suffering from dyslexia – but this made him doubly determined to succeed in an area of his own choosing in order to carve his own way in the world. International-level shooting and subsequently motor racing were to be his way out of isolation on a small-time Scottish filling station forecourt.

But it was more than that, more by far than three world championships won at the wheel of Ken Tyrrell's Matra and Tyrrell cars over the best part of a decade. The statistics clearly leave no doubt that he was a great driver, but study the dynamics of the situations he found himself in over the years and, truth be told, he was probably even better than he looked. The shorter wheelbase Tyrrells in which he gained much of his success during the final two seasons of his career were tricky cars in the extreme to drive quickly. Critics might also add that they weren't really very good. Yet Jackie's talent was such that he carried them to a level of success beyond their obvious potential. That was the ultimate measure of his status.

More than two decades after his retirement from driving, a Stewart-Ford F1 car driven by Johnny Herbert won the 1999 European GP at Nürburgring. By Jackie's own admission, it was a satisfying moment which came close to matching the emotion of his own visits to the F1 podium. And – as if to underline the fact that timing is everything in life – he sold the team to Ford at the end of that season.

7. BERND ROSEMEYER (Germany)

b. 14.10.1909, Lingen, Germany; d. 28.1.1938, nr Darmstadt, Germany

33 Grands Prix, 10 wins. Career span: 1935–37 (Auto Union).

Right, so it's moments like this which tax – and indeed question – one's sanity in tackling a book of this nature. You might think it distinctly unwise to stray outside the comfortable strictures and confines of the official F1 world championship, which of course started in 1950.

Yet this is a volume which deals with giants such as Gilles Villeneuve, Ronnie Peterson and Mario Andretti, men for whom words such as 'inspired' and 'dynamic' might have been specially coined. Bear that in mind and then ask how it's possible to overlook the brilliant Bernd Rosemeyer, the glittering and glamorous star of German motorsport who flashed across the horizon for three short seasons in the mid-1930s?

The son of a successful garage-owner, Rosemeyer began racing motorcycles at an early age and was quickly spotted and signed up by NSU and later DKW by 1934, after which it quickly became clear that he was an unusually talented young man at a time when the

Auto Union Grand Prix team was desperately short of drivers, with the honourable exception of Hans Stuck. At the end of that season, Auto Union therefore decided to invite twelve young drivers to the Nürburgring for an exhaustive test to establish whether any of them had any long-term potential. It quickly became clear that Rosemeyer was the most obvious talent among this promising group.

At the start of the 1935 season, Rosemeyer was invited to make his car racing debut for Auto Union at the super-fast Avus track near Berlin. It was the start of an action-packed year, full of spectacle and adventure, which added lustre to the legend of this young man who was quickly establishing a reputation as one of the most charismatic of German sportsmen. At the end of the '35 season he won the Czechoslovakian GP at Brno and, just as importantly, met the famous aviatrix Elly Beinhorn, who would soon become his wife.

British fans – including Tom Wheatcroft and commentating legend Murray Walker – recall watching at Donington Park as Rosemeyer opposite-locked his way to victory in the 1937 Grand Prix held at the parkland circuit near Derby. Wheatcroft, of course, would grow up to be a successful building contractor, and he later bought the track which in 1993 – 58 years after Rosemeyer's success – staged the European GP in conditions of torrential rain which helped Ayrton Senna to victory in a McLaren.

In the 1930s the business of record-breaking was a major priority within the German motorsport community, as success in this area was regarded as not only good for the car-maker concerned, but also a matter of national pride. In January 1938 both Auto Union and Mercedes-Benz turned out on the autobahn between Frankfurt and Darmstadt, where Rosemeyer was killed after losing control at over 270mph.

This national hero was buried with full military honours at Dahlem cemetery in Berlin and Elly was overwhelmed with thousands of letters of condolence, not simply written by Nazi leaders from Hitler down, but from fans across the world who identified with motor racing's first genuine international superstar.

6. JUAN-MANUEL FANGIO (Argentina)

b. 24.6.1911, Balcarce, Argentina; d. 17.7.1995, Balcarce

51 Grands Prix, 24 wins. World champion 1951, '54, '55, '56 and '57. Career span: 1950–51 (Alfa Romeo); 1953 (Maserati); 1954 (Maserati and Mercedes-Benz); 1955 (Mercedes-Benz); 1956 (Ferrari); 1958 (Maserati).

He was F1 racing's senior citizen, respected and revered as an icon from another era. Well into his eighties, his arrival in the pit lane was greeted with awe and reverential respect. Right to the end of his long life, Fangio was trim, dignified and radiated considerable presence.

This is not to say that Fangio was soft or over-sentimental. He was pragmatic; hard when he needed to be, but a sensitive and rather reserved gentleman away from the cockpit. He expected no favours and delivered few in return, but he had an overwhelming sense of sportsmanship and fair play. Although he was moved almost to tears by British driver Peter Collins's gesture in relinquishing his Lancia-Ferrari at Monza in 1956, by the same token there was no way he would ever offer a sliver of criticism in the direction of his other team-mate Luigi

Musso for failing to relinquish his steed.

Fangio was always shrewd. He won his first title crown for Alfa Romeo in 1951 as team-mate to the legendary Giuseppe Farina, and while his next title did not come until 1954 – a season split between Maserati and the dramatically returning Mercedes squad – he was always in contention, always a strong player that nobody could afford to ignore.

In 1955 he demonstrated both sensitivity and savvy when Stirling Moss, now his Mercedes team-mate, beat him by a length to win the British Grand Prix at Aintree. Fangio was clever enough never to suggest that he gifted Moss the win. But he never said he didn't either, thereby leaving an almost mystical quality surrounding Stirling's first championship success.

Later, in 1956, he would have something of a stressful and strained relationship with Enzo Ferrari, perhaps the least comfortable alliance of his professional racing career. From the touchlines many people felt that Fangio and the Commendatore were out of the same mould, in the sense that they had both achieved high status and respect within the motor racing community. Perhaps as a result each needed more in the way of deference and respect than the other was capable of delivering. They parted at the end of that season, but not before taking another title.

Yet at the end of the day it was the scale of Fangio's achievement which stood as the ultimate testimony to his unique genius. It is not the fact that Fangio won 24 Grands Prix which is so amazing – Jim Clark, Alain Prost, Niki Lauda, Ayrton Senna and Michael Schumacher all topped that total – but the fact that he did that in a career covering just 51 races.

That ensured that the serene man from the provincial Argentinian town won over 47 per cent of the Grands Prix he ever contested – a statistic which will almost certainly remain unmatched in F1 history.

5. ALBERTO ASCARI (Italy)

b. 13.7.1918, Turin; d. 26.5.1955, Monza

32 Grands Prix, 13 wins. World champion 1952 and '53. Career span: 1950–53 (Ferrari); 1954 (Maserati, Ferrari and Lancia); 1955 (Lancia).

One of Italy's favourite sons, Alberto Ascari was born into a motor racing family and is regarded as a greater driver than even the legendary Juan-Manuel Fangio who was his great contemporary and rival in the early 1950s. He was killed during an impromptu test of a Ferrari sports car at Monza, by coincidence on the same day of the same month as his father Antonio died contesting the 1926 French GP at Montlhéry. Indeed, an idiosyncratic sub-culture subsequently developed in an attempt to attach a deeper significance to these two unrelated facts.

Ascari's links with Ferrari went back to the very dawn of the company's existence. Enzo Ferrari had split with Alfa Romeo, whose racing programme he masterminded throughout the 1930s, on the very brink of the Second World War. Late in 1939 he was approached by two competitors who wanted him to build bespoke sports cars with which to contest the 1940 Mille Miglia road race. As a consequence of this commission, two eight-cylinder '815s' – as they were known, without any Ferrari branding – were commissioned by the young Ascari and the Marchese Lotario Rangoni Machievelli di

Modena, a well-heeled local aristocrat who was sadly destined to die in a wartime bomber crash.

Alberto's racing career began on motorcycles before he made the switch to four wheels, competing in that wartime Mille Miglia before racing shut down for the duration. By the end of the war, Ascari had a wife and children and so seriously considered giving up racing. But his old friend Luigi Villoresi persuaded him otherwise; they resumed together, driving a couple of Maseratis before switching to Ferrari the following season.

Ascari's domination of the 2-litre world championship in 1952 and '53 was total. Armed with the superb little Ferrari 500 he won the '52 European GP at Spa, then pretty much swept all before him through to the end of the following year. He then signed to drive the forthcoming new Lancia D50 the following year, but spent most of the season sitting on the sidelines twiddling his thumbs while the car was finally completed. The new Lancia was a highly sophisticated car with a powerful V8 engine and its fuel load carried partly in outriggers between the front and rear wheels on either side of the chassis, the better to enhance the D50's weight distribution. But by the middle of '54, Lancia was in financial trouble and the cost of F1 was seriously jeopardising the company's profitability.

Yet the Lancia D50 was an instantly competitive hit when it made its racing debut at the end of 1954. But Ascari had less time left than he could possibly imagine. He was poised to take the lead of the Monaco GP when he crashed spectacularly at the waterfront chicane and ended up taking a ducking in the harbour. The following week he was killed at Monza. He was a quiet, pleasant and universally popular man as well as a formidable competitor. It was left for Fangio to bestow the ultimate accolade. 'I have lost my greatest opponent,' he said quietly.

4. ALAIN PROST (France)

b. 24.2.1955, St Chamond, France

*199 Grands Prix, 51 wins. World champion 1985, '86, '89
and '93. Career span: 1980 (McLaren); 1981–83 (Renault);
1984–89 (McLaren); 1990–91 (Ferrari); 1993 (Williams).*

The faster he went, the slower he looked. Granted, that's
a gross oversimplification, but in essence this was the
unique quality about France's first-ever world champion.
Watching him shimmering from kerb to kerb with the
minimum of steering input, confident and unflustered in
pretty much equal measure, was to witness a masterclass
in F1 dynamics. Prost was good – very good indeed – as
I think his ranking within these pages undeniably
illustrates. But some would even rate him higher, perhaps
as the very best of all.

Alain freely admitted that when he joined McLaren
in 1984 alongside Niki Lauda this was indeed a dream
come true. It was alongside the Austrian that he fully
matured as a driver, honing his meticulous style as he
learned everything the Austrian could teach him.
Moreover, the new TAG turbo-engined McLaren proved
to be the class of the field, but although Alain won seven
races and Niki only five, it was the Austrian who clinched
the championship by the narrowest margin ever – just
half a point.

In 1985 Prost made no mistakes, winning five races
to take the championship at last. More significantly,
he retained the crown in '86, thus becoming the first
driver to win consecutive championships since Jack
Brabham in 1959–60. In 1987 another record came his
way; after hounding Gerhard Berger's Ferrari into a spin

during the Portuguese GP at Estoril, Prost surged past the chequered flag to beat Jackie Stewart's thirteen-year record of 27 wins.

Then in 1988, Prost found himself facing the biggest challenge of his career when Ayrton Senna was signed to drive alongside him and the team switched to Honda power for what was to be the final year of the turbo engine regulations. The combination of these two great drivers and the new McLaren-Honda conferred such an advantage over the opposition that the two men turned the world championship into their own personal playground, winning fifteen out of the sixteen races.

Prost was forced to raise the standard of his game to keep on terms with his young, thrusting team-mate. Even so, he took fewer calculated gambles in traffic than Ayrton and increasingly found it impossible to conceal his dislike of racing in the rain. But he still managed to bag his third world championship in '89 before leaving the team and switching to Ferrari.

He came close to polishing off a fourth title crown in 1991, but after he was rammed off the track by Senna's McLaren on the first corner at Suzuka his already brittle relationship with Ferrari never quite fully recovered, because they obviously felt he had been insufficiently defensive. Alain stayed with the Scuderia through to the end of 1992 when he was controversially fired with one race to go. Understandably, he was taken aback by his treatment from the Maranello brigade and opted for a year's sabbatical in 1992. Then he returned with Williams for one last blast in '93, taking his fourth world championship at the age of 38. By any standards, it had been quite a career.

3. AYRTON SENNA (Brazil)

b. 21.3.1960, São Paolo, Brazil; d. 1.5.1994, Bologna

161 Grands Prix, 41 wins. World champion 1988, '90 and '91. Career span: 1984 (Toleman); 1985–87 (Lotus); 1988–93 (McLaren); 1994 (Williams).

Of all the leading lights in this compendium, Senna lays claim to a high rating by virtue not only of his towering skill behind the wheel but also by reason of the messianic zeal and self-belief which was the powerhouse of his restless ambition. Ayrton won his first world championship for McLaren in 1988, but this was merely a staging post on a longer journey which brought him two more titles in 1990 and '91 before he was killed when his Williams FW16 crashed while leading the 1994 San Marino GP at Imola.

Ron Dennis, the McLaren boss, got an early insight into what made Senna tick. At the end of the 1982 season the young Brazilian was considering his options for graduating into the British Formula 3 championship for the following year. Dennis, astutely realising the calibre of this new boy, offered to fund his season in this crucial junior category in exchange for a long-term option on his services. Senna declined, preferring to keep his options open. He won the F3 title and then made the move into F1 with the Toleman team in 1984.

Senna never took anything for granted, or indeed left anything to chance. When he signed his Toleman contract he shrewdly negotiated a release clause whereby he could leave the team if it failed to produce a competitive package. For 1985 he decided to invoke that clause and moved up the ladder to Lotus. There was nothing personal or vindictive about his decision; he merely wanted to do the best for his career development. After three years with Lotus he decided his greater experience again merited a better team, so he moved again, this time to McLaren. It was precisely the right move at the right moment.

Moving to McLaren as team-mate to Alain Prost, the team's 'sitting tenant', looked like a huge challenge to confront. But Senna was in no way intimidated by the magnitude of the task before him. He would, he told his colleagues, out-perform Prost by being quicker, fitter and more determined. He was as good as his word, winning eight races to Prost's seven during the course of the '88 season and clinching his first championship.

In 1989 the rivalry between the two men reached fever pitch. There was a major row when Prost accused Senna of reneging on a 'no passing' agreement on the opening lap of the San Marino GP at Imola. Ron Dennis had to draw on all his resources of diplomacy to heal the breach between his two men, but the trouble exploded again at Suzuka where the two McLarens collided as they battled for the lead of the Japanese GP.

Prost emerged champion after this very public debacle while Senna, who was disqualified from the Suzuka race after restarting and crossing the finishing line first, got himself into more hot water by making some incautious observations about the FIA president Jean-Marie Balestre. Yet that was Ayrton all over; he would never shirk from doing what he judged was best for himself. That philosophy led him to join Williams at the start of 1994; it was a partnership which promised great things but which was brutally torn asunder before it could catch its stride.

2. JIM CLARK (Great Britain)

b. 4.3.1936, Kilmany, Fife, Scotland; d. 7.4.1968,
Hockenheim

*72 Grands Prix, 25 wins. World champion 1963 and '65.
Career span: 1960–68 (Lotus).*

There are still those within the motorsport community
who believe that Clark – always 'Jimmy' to his legions of
devoted fans – should head this list as number one. I
quite understand that viewpoint, but must confess that
when I originally compiled this list I placed the legendary
Scot only fourth.

On reflection, that ranking was simply not high
enough. When Clark died in a minor league F2 race at
Hockenheim in the spring of 1968, the whole fabric of
international motor racing trembled. Clark, more than
anybody else in the history of the sport, had seemed
totally inviolate. And in my humble opinion he scored
what still stands out as the most impressive single victory
in the record books, the 1963 Belgian Grand Prix at
Spa-Francorchamps.

Think about it. The old Spa track was a daunting 8.749
miles long, over public roads through the pine forests of
the Haute Fagnes region, and the rain poured down
relentlessly. No matter. The incomparable Clark lapped
the entire field in his Lotus, slowing down only in the
closing stages to permit Bruce McLaren's second-place
Cooper to unlap itself before the chequered flag.

This gets the nomination as my greatest race simply
because Clark exerted a level of dominance in the
appalling conditions that eclipsed everything else he
achieved, even in his illustrious career. To be eight miles

ahead of your nearest rival in rain and spray on a track lined by walls, farm buildings and telegraph poles was a simply momentous achievement.

Clark was a rather shy, self-effacing son of a Scottish border farmer who went motor racing primarily for his own pleasure. In so many ways he was the last great sporting 'amateur' driver, and he died just before the onset of unbridled commercialism – which he abhorred – in the sport he loved so passionately.

The record books show he won the world championship in 1963 and '65, but came within a whisker of taking it in '62 and '64 as well. The fact of the matter is that he dominated all four seasons in a manner seldom matched since. The green Lotus with its yellow stripe and blue-helmeted driver won a total of 25 Grands Prix between 1962 and his death six years later, yet it was the manner of Clark's success which really demoralised his opposition.

Inevitably starting from pole position, he would destroy his competitors' spirit with a searing first lap which none of them could approach, let alone equal. He was the yardstick by which his contemporaries judged their own performance, and he had most of them psychologically beaten before they even climbed into their cars.

Clark also took time out to contest the Indianapolis 500 classic US oval race, competing for the first time in 1963 – when he finished second – and then missing the clashing Monaco GP to win the famous American event two years later. Jimmy proved every bit as adept in tackling the specialised techniques required on oval circuits as he was at the wheel of an F1 car. By any standards, he was the complete driver.

1. STIRLING MOSS (Great Britain)

b. 17.9.1929, London

*66 Grands Prix, 16 wins. Career span: 1952 (HWM, ERA
and Connaught); 1953 (Connaught and Cooper); 1954, 1956
(Maserati); 1955 (Mercedes); 1957 (Maserati and Vanwall);
1958 (Vanwall and Cooper); 1960 (Cooper and Lotus); 1961
(Lotus).*

Tricky one, this. OK, I can hear you say. But how on
earth do you justify Stirling's position at the pinnacle of
this elite list when assessed against multiple world
champions including Michael Schumacher, Ayrton Senna
and Alain Prost? After all, Moss's list of F1 achievement
looks positively modest alongside some of the newer
additions to the sport's hall of fame. So how does this
logic all stack up?

Well, let's just consider the accident which ended his
career at Goodwood on Easter Monday, 1962. After
Stirling crashed his UDT-Laystall team Lotus during
the non-championship Glover Trophy, the entire country
waited with baited breath as he lay unconscious in
his hospital bed for almost a month. For Moss had
long since come to be regarded as a national institution,
not only one of the UK's foremost international
sportsmen but a huge personality in his own right, a
character who radiated infectious enthusiasm and huge
charisma.

After serving an apprenticeship in the junior formulae,
Moss emerged as one of the country's undisputed rising
stars, to the point where his father Alfred and his
manager Ken Gregory sounded out Mercedes-Benz to
see whether the legendary German car-maker might be

interested in pairing Stirling with Juan-Manuel Fangio for the marque's F1 return in 1954.

Mercedes team manager Alfred Neubauer was interested, but wanted to see how Moss handled a fully-fledged F1 car before making such a far-reaching commitment. As a result, with generous financial support from BP, Moss acquired a Maserati 250F for the 1954 season and set out to prove his talent to Neubauer. By the time the young British driver had dominated the Italian GP at Monza, pulling away from Fangio's Mercedes before the Maserati stopped with fading oil pressure, Neubauer was fully convinced. He duly signed Stirling for 1955 and Moss repaid that confidence by winning the British GP at Aintree.

In 1956 Moss was back to Maserati, now a member of the factory team, and then for 1957 finally realised his life's ambition by driving for Tony Vandervell's famous Vanwall squad. Here at last was the British potential world championship-winner which Moss dreamed of. It almost carried him to the sport's pinnacle the following year, Moss losing out only by a single point to his Ferrari-mounted rival Mike Hawthorn. With Vanwall withdrawing from the fray at the end of 1958, for the balance of his career the British star switched to Rob Walker's private team, memorably scoring the Lotus marque's maiden victory in the 1960 Monaco GP.

For 1961, the first year of the 1.5-litre F1 regulations, Moss continued driving the Walker Lotus, posting seminal victories at Monaco – his third – and the Nürburgring. There were plans afoot for him to drive a Walker-entered Ferrari for the '62 title chase, but those were scuppered in the twisted wreck against the bank at Goodwood. Years later, Stirling would concede that he'd retired too soon. Had he gone head-to-head with Jimmy Clark through the mid-

1960s, who knows what great deeds we might have witnessed.

CONCLUSION

There are, or have been, too many good Grand Prix drivers, particularly when you are trying to trim the list down to this level. Why no Giancarlo Baghetti, the only man to have won a maiden GP victory? Answer, because the Italian wasn't good enough, even though he got lucky in the broiling heat at Reims one afternoon in 1961. Others who fail to make it include my good friends Jackie Oliver and Peter Gethin, even though Peter won the '71 Italian GP at an average speed of 150mph, but the balance of their front-line careers were too patchy and inconsistent.

On the other hand, you might be forgiven for thinking that Brian Redman's inclusion in the top 100 is a little too historically speculative, but I would contend that the qualities which made him such a rounded sports car ace were obviously also a factor in his fleeting F1 involvements.

As far as wider, far-reaching conclusions are concerned, there are none. This volume represents a snapshot of hopes fulfilled and broken dreams. An everyday story about F1 people, in fact.

MARK HUGHES

LEWIS
HAMILTON
THE FULL STORY

'The one Lewis book which people who love racing should read'

James Allen

'Don't be duped into thinking the official book will automatically be the best option. *The Full Story* is a far better choice.'

F1Fanatic.co.uk

'Written with insider knowledge, and that fact shows through'

Autosport

'This has more incisive analysis of his success than the official version and, weirdly, greater detail on his early racing career.'

Observer

'Provides more detail, particularly on the earliest days of his racing career, than Hamilton's own version ... the volume for the petrolhead in your life.'

Daily Telegraph

THE
GRAND PRIX COMPANION

1906

'Anybody who has even a passing interest in this spectacular sport will find something to absorb them in this book.'

NIKI LAUDA

- ALAN HENRY -

'A unique insight into the sport ... a must read for anybody whose juices flow at the prospect of F1.'

Sunday Times, Book of the Week

'Henry sounds a thoroughly amusing companion, and he has written a very entertaining one as well.'

Independent on Sunday, Book of the Week

'This nuggety publication is crammed with fact, reminiscence, opinion and trivia ... I enjoyed [it] very much.'

Daily Telegraph

' A tome no sensible Grand Prix fan will want to miss.'

Autocar

'A user-friendly miscellany that bristles with facts, figures and anecdotes. Poignant in parts. Delightful throughout.'

Motorsport Magazine

'Alan Henry is a real authority in the sport and has been around long enough to get behind the visor of every driver worth talking about. The whole book is written with enthusiasm and genuine affection. It reads like a conversation in a pub and, before you know it, it'll be closing time.'

BBC *Top Gear Magazine*, Book of the Month